SCOTLAND

SCOTLAND

PHOTOGRAPHED BY DOUGLAS CORRANCE
WITH TEXT BY MAGNUS LINKLATER

COLLINS
GLASGOW AND LONDON

For my parents,
Malcolm and Mary Corrance

Designed by Westpoint, Glasgow

Published by William Collins Sons and Company Limited
Photographs © Scottish Tourist Board
Text © William Collins Sons and Company Limited
First published 1984

Printed in Great Britain
ISBN 0 00 435677 2

Scotland's for me!

INTRODUCTION

Fifty years ago the Orkney poet Edwin Muir set out in a battered 1921 Standard motor car to travel round Scotland. He drove south from Edinburgh, crossing the Borders from east to west, then turned north, through Glasgow to the Highlands. Finally, breathing a sigh of relief, he crossed the Pentland Firth back to his native islands.

It was not a happy journey. Muir was infinitely depressed by what he saw as a country in decline. "Scotland," he mourned, "is gradually being emptied of its population, its spirit, its wealth, industry, art, intellect and innate character." He was particularly pessimistic about the Lowlands and the big cities: "Industry itself is vanishing like a dream . . . a large population lives there in idleness, for there is nowhere else to go, and little prospect that Monday will dawn for a long time."

Muir's Scottish journey was made in the grim conditions of the 1930s. He was in a black mood when he began it and a blacker one when he had finished. Yet as he nursed his temperamental little car clockwise around the country, Muir the poet kept on interrupting Muir the social commentator. Despite his stern intention to reach the bleakest conclusions about Scotland, he kept on being side-tracked.

He was exhilarated by the street life of Edinburgh, the sturdy independence of the Border towns, and the splendour of the Highlands. There were communities and villages where the message of doom appeared to have had remarkably little impact, even if it had been heard at all. By the time he reached the north, he was reserving most of his irritation for his struggling little motor car, which was encountering grave difficulties on the gradients of Sutherland, rather than the self-destruction of the nation. Scotland, in short, was refusing – as always – to conform to a stereotype. It is a lesson which most travellers in the country have learned in time, however well tuned their prejudices may have been to begin with. And it is one which this book again confirms.

Douglas Corrance, whose journeys across Scotland over the past ten years have yielded the splendid and varied photographs which follow, would not, for a moment, pretend to any fixed prejudice about his country beyond a great enjoyment of it, and a serious conviction that it contains more wealth in terms of its people and the places they live in than most outsiders dream of. He is aware – as his pictures often and wittily demonstrate – that it has its absurdities; and he is only too conscious of the banality which surrounds so much of the tourist's image of Scotland. But in the end he finds he likes the place enormously. As a photographer who has worked often abroad, he discovers more inspiration in Scotland than anywhere else, and these pictures reflect it. He calls them "a celebration".

Which, in 1984, may seem surprising. Scotland today is in the grip of a recession that is, in many respects, more severe, more durable, more insidiously damaging even than the one which Edwin Muir chronicled so gloomily in 1934. With unemployment hovering around the 15 per cent mark, leaving nearly 350,000 Scots men and women on the dole; with the great oil boom, which seemed once to offer so much, rapidly receding; and with the surge of confidence, which devolution held out, now only a fading dream, Scotland's prospects might well appear every bit as depressing as they were to Muir. Certainly the steady drift south of the country's best brains, which led him to complain caustically that "its large towns are composed of astute capitalists and angry proletarians, with nothing that matters much in between", has continued, and, if anything, speeded up.

And yet, as Corrance's pictures repeatedly testify, there is no absence of vigour, enterprise and sheer native vitality to be recorded up and down the land. His journey, unlike Muir's, is anticlockwise. It begins, sensibly enough, in the southeast where the traveller from England first crosses into Scotland, then meanders gently northwards across Border country to Edinburgh. As a photographer, he is struck by the clean images of the lowland countryside where the hills are rounded and the rich arable land neatly patterned by the ruthless efficiency of the Border farmers. He finds many of the old lowland traditions alive and well – the Border Ridings, the Beltane Festival, Guid Nychburris Day, the Braw Lad's Gathering. Although heavily adapted to the 20th century and the voracious demands of the tourist, they each retain their individuality – as do the Border towns like Kelso where outwardly little seems to have changed but where a certain canniness is evident in the way new industries have been lured in to shore up employment.

In Edinburgh, as later in Glasgow, it is the people who catch the eye of the camera. The truculence of a kilted sergeant-major, the firm but friendly waitress mothering her customers, the faintly absurd but resolutely dignified elders processing in an annual ceremony – these would have been instantly recognizable to any Edinburgh visitor at any time over the past hundred years. They give an immediate sense of the life and character of the city – something even Edwin Muir noted and warmed to. Some twenty years later, George Scott-Moncrieff concluded: "He who comes to Edinburgh has to bring his own responsiveness, and then I think he will rarely be disappointed." Corrance has certainly done that, and Edinburgh has given back in like measure. For those who complain that his camera has averted its eye from the down-at-heel wynds or the drug addicts or the dole queues or the insensitive redevelopment which are also part of modern Edinburgh, the answer is that it is responding here to a different kind of image – something harder to define than social decline, but nearer perhaps to the true nature of the city. Distortion? I don't think so. Corrance just happens to like the place. He sees the best in it, not the worst. And he photographs it that way.

At the same time, he has a neat way of highlighting the more ludicrous habits of the Scots, particularly when they are aping their own traditions. He can poke fun at the mini-kilts of the girls twirling batons in a parody of old Scottish ceremony, and he can puncture the pomposity of a group of lawyers in their 18th-century garb. The affection of the Scots themselves for the tinsel travesties of their history has been the despair of generations of Scottish writers. The triumph of tartan and Tannochbrae, of Bonnie Prince Charlie and Rabbie Burns, of sword dances and haggis and hairy sporrans, has come about not just because the tourists want them, but because the Scots themselves are addicted. And they have been for a long time. Most modern historians would trace the origins of all this Scottish "kitsch" back to the 19th century and the wilting of an indigenous Scottish culture. They dismiss it as mawkish, parochial and degenerate – what the historian William Ferguson calls "ben and glen" romanticism. But Tom Nairn, whose book *The Break-Up of Britain* contains a typically radical analysis of the "Kailyard" (literally "cabbage patch") tradition in Scotland, points out that this "vast tartan monster" is anything but feeble: "Most intellectuals – and nationalists chief amongst them – have flinched away from him, dismissing the beast over-easily as mere proof of the debased condition of a nation without a State of its own. It is far more important, surely, to study this insanely sturdy sub-culture. Tartanry will not wither away, if only because it possesses the force of its own vulgarity – immunity from doubt and higher culture. Whatever form of self-rule Scotland acquires, this is a substantial part of the real inheritance bequeathed to it."

There is, as the journey proceeds, a certain amount of fun to be had with the tartan beast. There are the upper classes disporting themselves at Highland balls, and the other classes indulging in the rituals of the Highland Games. Campbells pour into the Castle at Inveraray to make sure that clan supremacy is still alive and well, and the astonishing Burns industry grinds on fifty years after Edwin Muir complained about the hordes of people queuing up at his cottage, "wandering about the courtyard behind the bars like tame animals". This, he said, "was exactly what the cult of Burns worship was bound to turn into in a commercialised, newspaper-reading, bus-driven, cinema-educated age ... the best thing would be for the whole nation reluctantly and reverently to pull the poet's birthplace down, on a day of decent mourning . . ." Today, in a television-saturated age, there is no sign that the nation shows any inclination to take his advice to heart.

Pursuing this irreverent bent, Douglas Corrance gently sends up some of the more cherished images of romantic Scotland. Eilean Donan Castle, which has graced more biscuit-box lids than any other building in Scotland, is pictured disappearing into an impossible sunset, and a group of Highland cattle look more like creatures from some gothic horror film than those cuddly creatures who usually peer out at us from the picture postcards of Mr J. Arthur Dixon. There is, it has to be said, a certain ambivalence about Corrance's attitude. He can out-do Mr Dixon any day, and on occasion does. Thus, another group of heavily fringed Highland cattle, knee deep in the waters of Loch Lomond under a deep blue sky, may well be a parody – or are they posing for next year's bestselling postcard?

It would, however, be quite misleading to suggest that this is the main thrust of the book. As we move north through the harbour villages of Fife to the great castles of Aberdeenshire, and on to the Highlands, there are constant and brooding reminders of Scotland's history. A certain recurrence of stark ruins or bleak battlefields does not betray anything so complex as an obsession with the past; they are there because they make splendid pictures, and no one travelling through Scotland can or should ignore them. Besides, they are an essential part of the business of understanding the place.

But anyone attempting to acquire a rudimentary grasp of Scottish history by reading the captions – for which I am responsible – will be looking in the wrong place. The information they contain is highly selective. Just as the camera is constantly diverted from any serious message by an arresting image or an amusing juxtaposition of people and places, so I have leaned towards descriptions which are diverting rather than educational. The balance of them is towards a general theme which might roughly be termed the Survival of Scotland – surviving, as it often has, by its wits. If there is one new industry to have properly emerged since Edwin Muir so sourly travelled north, it is tourism, and the Scots have thrown themselves into it with enthusiasm.

From stately homes to wildlife parks and skiing resorts, to fishing, pony trekking and climbing centres, and on down to the tiniest bed-and-breakfast cottage, one gains an over-riding impression of a country exploring every available resource to transform itself into a tourist trap.

It is at least partly this that explains how the harbour villages of the east coast, where the fishing industry is in a near-terminal state, look more freshly painted and sprightly than they have for decades, There is little sign of depression or decay, although the visitor will often find more pleasure craft than fishing boats crowding the harbours. Elsewhere, restoration seems to be more in vogue than at any time since 1660: ancient dukes have managed to spruce up their ancient castles, thanks to the streams of tourists prepared to part with large sums of money for the privilege of seeing how dukes used to – and very often still do – exist. Small towns like Dunkeld in Perthshire or Culross in Fife have been brought back from a state of crumbling ruin to pristine shape; they probably look better now than they did two hundred years ago. And, in the most unlikely places – the tiny Ross-shire village of Achiltibuie, for instance – hotels and inns have been retrieved from that despairing state of brown panelling, linoleum floors and bleak rice puddings into which the Scottish catering trade seemed at one time to have been frozen for ever.

Scotland, in short, has become a thriving tourist state. But at what cost? It is in the course of descending in a leisurely manner down the northwest coast of Scotland, venturing out to Lewis and the Uists, taking in Skye, the Summer Isles, Ullapool and Mallaig, that the camera and the social commentator find themselves most at odds. The camera is naturally seduced by the glories of the Highland coast, its colours, its sky, its endlessly beguiling sunsets and its outrageously romantic hills. And this, too, is why the summer visitors are there. But what has happened in the meantime to the lives of the Highlanders? Tourism is a cyclical and strictly limited industry. It can sustain a village for six months in the year, but then it moves on and out, abandoning its part-time host to real life. And what does that amount to? It is fifty years since Hugh MacDiarmid, another jaundiced observer of the Scottish scene, wrote the following passage: "Certainly while petty emotionalism may revel in glories of gold and mysterious purples, a little reflection on the real life round our coasts – on the derelict harbours and ruined fishing villages, on the wanton destruction of the old island economy, on the devastation wrought by English and other foreign trawlers, on the forced emigration and progressive depopulation of the Highlands and Islands, on the general lack of knowledge and certainly the extreme rarity of first-hand and detailed knowledge of the conditions of fishing and crofting life, or the fact that the hardships of the weather and a meagre living are nothing to the preventible hardships of Governmental oppression and neglect, and on the fact that other parts of Europe even less favourably circumstanced than the lonliest wastal stretches on any of the islands of Scotland, and under far greater natural handicaps, are able to maintain their traditional industry in a flourishing condition while ours is going steadily from bad to worse – must prove sobering enough to anyone who has the interests of Scotland at heart."

Now, after allowing for MacDiarmid's polemic, not to mention the formidable length of his sentences, it would be hard to claim that things have changed greatly for the better since he wrote that. The progressive depopulation of the Highlands has continued. The staple industries of crofting and fishing have steadily declined, despite the single-minded efforts of such bodies as the Highlands and Islands Development Board. The coastal waters off Ullapool, for instance, are strewn each season with the insatiable factory ships of Bulgaria, Poland and other East European countries, which come to purchase and process the west coast mackerel. The rate at which they are doing so will – unless catches are limited – lead as inevitably to the extinction of the mackerel stock as over-fishing destroyed the herring industry a decade ago. Efforts to set up light industries, or even heavier ones, such as the pulp mills at Fort William, have too often fallen victim to the national state of economic decline, as well, perhaps, as to a certain West Highland fatalism. Of course there have been success stories, but all in all, it is as easy to be gloomy about the prospects for the Highlands today as MacDiarmid was in 1934.

There are occasional glimpses in Douglas Corrance's pictures of this decline – a deserted croft in Sutherland, for instance, harks back, not to the Clearances but to a more recent emigration. That, however, is not his main business. Instead he has chosen to picture the people of the crofting communities who have remained, defying the gloomiest of MacDiarmid's predictions, and retaining – in smaller communities perhaps, and certainly in smaller numbers overall – the essential character of the west coast. Anyone who knows and loves the Highlands will recognize his lady at the petrol pump, or the gentlemen on Mallaig pier, stomach to stomach, discussing the topics of the day.

"They are a great race;" wrote an English enthusiast, Brooke Heckstall

Smith, "they always have been a grand people; and if modern times will let them, will remain so; a race of men and women which has survived the centuries in this Highland land, among barren hills and wild seas, of storms and raging winters, or famine and battle and murder, must of necessity be a hardy race; it is not a land where any but the fittest can survive, year in, year out. One cannot have any feeling except of the deepest respect for such a people and I wish we Sassenachs, as a body, would remember these things when we visit, talk to, or write about our Highland hosts, for as such I regard them when we intrude on their territories."

The warmth of that regard is reflected in this book, and extends from the Highlands south to the far reaches of Galloway and Wigtownshire as Corrance's journey reaches its end. He winds up as far away from Edwin Muir's native Orkney as it is possible to get, and his mood at the finish could hardly be more different. Yet there is a meeting point. At the conclusion of his book, Muir makes an impassioned plea for an economic revolution in Scotland which would give it a greater measure of independence than it has had since the Union with England in 1707. He is not arguing for Scottish Nationalism, but he does have a view of a society which can take pride in its own achievements and realize its national potential without subservience to its southern neighbour. "There is no doubt," he writes, "that the Scottish people, with their immense store of potential energy, would be capable of using the resources of modern production to create a society such as I have imagined . . . Scotland has no future save through such a chance. This view may seem at first a depressing one, but to me it seems the only cheerful one."

Here, at last, the two journeys coincide, for in the course of his celebration of Scotland, Douglas Corrance also reflects both its "immense store of potential energy" and the determined ability of its people to defy the direst predictions for their future. The book, then, is a testimonial not only to the beauty of Scotland but also to its sturdiness. It emphasizes the qualities that make it a country greatly loved by those who were born and brought up within its borders, and fiercely defended by those who have long since left it. Corrance has chosen to see it – often literally – in its best light; and neither he, nor I, would make any apology for that.

Magnus Linklater, Riemore, 1984

Smailholm Tower in Roxburghshire,
a sturdy 16th-century Border keep,
stands out against the background
of a winter's sunset. Walter Scott
brought Turner here, and he drew it
in a rather absurd, romantic style;
but he may have been encouraged
by Scott who claims he sat here as a
boy and conjured up visions of
Scotland's mighty past:
"Methought that still with trump
   and clang,
The gateway's broken arches rang;
Methought grim features, seam'd
   with scars,
Glared through the window's rusty
   bars . . ."

The harbour master at Eyemouth on the Berwickshire coast, just north of the border with England, has some twenty-five boats to supervise. They fish off the Lothian coast, and unlike some of the ports farther north, they do good business. The calm waters of the harbour and the blue sky above are far removed from the worst day in Eyemouth's history when, in 1881, the entire fishing fleet was wrecked within sight of the shore by a freak storm, and half of Eyemouth's families were left without fathers or husbands. In Eyemouth today there is a fisheries museum, opened in 1981 – the centenary of that terrible disaster.

The dying minutes of an autumn evening on the Tweed; the dedicated angler, casting downstream, has no eyes for the majestic sunset he is about to miss. This may be the most promising part of the day, and as the stream takes his fly, the full force of his concentration will be on its bouncing progress. The Tweed has the latest season of any salmon river in Scotland – it goes on until 30 November, when there are still fresh-run fish to be caught. But by that time many of the salmon may be "red" – that is, they are dark coloured from having been in the river all summer – and in the time of Alexander I the catching of red fish was strongly disapproved of. In the 12th century he ordered that "Slayers of reide or smoltes of salmond, the third time are punished by death"

Beneath the Eildon Hills, the River Tweed has almost formed a perfectly circular island where, as everywhere in the Borders, the spare acres are devoted to grazing.

The Eildon Hills have long been the focus for legend, the most famous being that of Thomas the Rhymer whose three years spent there consorting with the Queen of the Fairies is chronicled in a marvellous 15th-century poem full of sexual innuendo, much of which was sanitized in later versions, particularly the lines where the Queen commands Thomas to lay his head on her knee:
"And thou shall see the fayrest syghte
That ever sawe mane of this contree."

Snow encircling St Mary's Loch, Selkirkshire, where Wordsworth once noted
"The swan on still St Mary's Lake
Float double, swan and shadow."
It still has a remote and enchanting quality, quite different from the forbidding bleakness of the rugged Border hills to the west. On the isthmus that separates St Mary's Loch from its neighbour, the Loch of the Lowes, stands one of Scotland's more celebrated literary inns, Tibbie Shiel's, whose associations with Scott, De Quincey, Lockhart, and James Hogg, the Ettrick Shepherd, made it *the* place to stop at on the way north.

To the ordinary passer-by these pictures will say something of the timeless quality of agricultural life: the dilatory flock of sheep comprehensively blocking a country road; wintering ewes chewing steadily on turnips; cows dotted on a green velvet field.

To the expert they will say more about the stern efficiency of farming in the Borders where, over the past ten years, there has been a minor agricultural revolution. Common Market policies have encouraged a swing from stock to arable farming, with many additional acres coming under the plough. Technical advances have increased yields dramatically – from an average of thirty-two hundredweight to around three tons an acre. At the same time, the Border hill farms with their blackfaced sheep have been rescued from the economic disaster that so recently threatened them. Lower down, greyfaced sheep, less hardy but more productive, are fed through the winter on turnips until they can be fattened up on the spring grass for the summer sales. Dairy farms are less common, but those that do exist are run with great efficiency and a canny eye to profit. All in all,

the Borders are thriving.

But to the photographer these images simply said: good colour and perfect composition. As Douglas Corrance points out, "The fact that the cows all faced in the same direction was a great bonus. Just one facing the other way round would have ruined it."

The marketplace of Kelso in Roxburghshire (above), reflected in an old-fashioned, chemist's flask. The symbol may be appropriate – Kelso is probably the best preserved of the Border towns. But it is very far from being a museum piece. In fact, the town is one of the fastest expanding in the area. An active town council has lured industry including plastics, electronics, knitwear and a bottling plant; there is an industrial estate; and there is the tourist trade. As a result, Kelso's population has grown by more than 25 per cent over the past ten years and held unemployment at bay despite the recession. Another example of Border efficiency.

There is nothing particularly handsome or salutary about a jail, however ancient. This one at Jedburgh (above right), built on the site of the old castle in 1823, reminds one how little prisons have altered in the last hundred years or so. Even the slopping-out pail and the peepholes in the cell doors remain essentially the same. Jedburgh, the former county town of Roxburghshire, was famous, or infamous, for a principle known as Jeddart Justice, whereby a person was held to be guilty until proved innocent. A robber would thus be hanged first and tried later. But that predated the jail.

In the grounds of Dryburgh Abbey lie memorials to three not entirely flawless Scottish heroes: James II (depicted here on the right), blown up by one of his own cannons during the siege of Roxburgh Castle in 1460; Sir Walter Scott, who died defeated by the overwhelming odds of his financial debts; and Earl Haig, whose generalship in the First World War finally secured victory but at an appalling cost in human lives.

A short walk to the banks of the Jed leads one to the melancholy splendour of Jedburgh Abbey, best preserved of the Border abbeys but a ruin nevertheless. All of them – Melrose, Dryburgh and Jedburgh – were destroyed by English invasion, and the villain in each case was the Earl of Hertford who wrecked all three (Melrose twice) and left their stones to be picked up and used over the years by local builders. Standing in the south aisle and nave of Jedburgh, beneath the rose window which remains, one can see something of the confidence of Scotland's independent church. It was at least partly this that provoked so massive a destruction.

The strange statue on the left, the Black Dwarf, stands in the garden of a cottage in Kirkton Manor near Peebles. The cottage was the home of "Bowed David Ritchie", only three feet six inches tall, on whom Scott based his novel *The Black Dwarf*. The cottage has a special "dwarf" door.

It would be unthinkable to visit the Border country of Walter Scott without paying homage to Abbotsford, the house he bought himself and transformed from the once modestly named Clartyhole into the great Border seat of a great Border laird, thus cementing art and life into one improbable edifice. Abbotsford is not to everyone's taste. Edwin Muir described it as "This pompous, crude, fantastic, unmanageable, heartless, insatiable, comfortless brute of a house". Still lived in by Scott descendants, it is also a museum, the contents assembled by Scott himself with near manic determination. He gathered under one roof almost as many of the artefacts of Scottish history as, in his literary career, he assembled in his novels. Thus you may inspect Burns's whisky glass, Rob Roy's claymore, etc., etc. And into Scott's death mask you may read the contradictions and, perhaps, the disappointments of a life which was rich but fell short of his own expectations. Yet, as A.N. Wilson pointed out recently, Scott was a superstar: "Even by the standards of the time Scott was distinct. The Victorians canonised him."

Borderers take their customs and traditions seriously, particularly the annual Riding of the Marches (or borders), though time and the demands of tourism have led to a little muddling over the years. The Beltane Festival in Peebles (above left), for example, which goes back into the dim reaches of early history and was a ritual held on the eve of 1 May, is now combined with the annual Riding which dates back to the 17th century and is held in June. Thomas Pennant, who travelled through Scotland in 1769, described how the Beltane Cake was used as a symbol to protect stock and crops during the coming year. Everyone would break off a piece and throw it over their shoulders, saying "This I give to thee, preserve thou my horses; this to thee, preserve thou my sheep," and so on. Things have changed a little since then.

In Dumfries (above right) the Riding is held on "Guid Nychburris Day", literally Good Neighbours' Day. The ceremony was first recorded in 1641, but is almost certainly older. These days it is a week-long festival with the leaders of the processions (known as Cornet and Cornet's Lass) taking on the roles of ambassadors, touring other festivals and representing the town. Far from dying out, the whole affair has taken on a new lease of life.

In Galashiels it is the "Braw Lads' Gathering" (opposite above), but the idea is the same. There is, as you may note, an element of the middle-class gymkhana about it, but a good time is had by all. The actual title comes from a poem by Burns, "The Braw Lads of Galla Water", and although the festival's antecedents are obscure, it too goes back to the days when marking out the boundaries of a burgh was not only prudent but enjoined by law.

A more serious tradition by far, and one whose rules are a great deal stricter, is the Border Sevens – the seven-a-side rugby competition which established the supremacy of Gala, Hawick, Kelso or any of the other Border clubs which enter (opposite below, Selkirk v Kelso). From here come the men who form the heart of Scotland's national fifteen, and if that team has known greater days, its time will doubtless come again.

21

There are three important points to be noted about Traquair House in Peeblesshire, which may account for the superior look on the face of the King Charles spaniel lying in front of it. The first is that it is said to be the oldest continually inhabited house in Scotland; the second is that its old gates have not been opened since 1745; and the third is that Traquair has its own brewery and markets its own beer.

Continuous inhabitation is, of course, notoriously hard to prove, and only one small part of the house (the 10th-century northeast tower) dates back beyond Charles I; but the first assertion has so far fought off all challengers. The second is a matter of some dispute. The popular story is that the gates were closed in 1745, following a visit by Bonnie Prince Charlie, and will not be opened again until a Stuart monarch sits once more on the throne. But there is a rival claim: that they were shut after the death of a countess of Traquair whose husband vowed they should stay closed until another countess should enter. His successor died unmarried, which means that we shall have to use the side entrance for some time to come. The third point is incontestable: the beer at Traquair is excellent.

Floors Castle, in Roxburghshire, claims another record: the largest inhabited mansion in Scotland, and no one contemplating this vast turreted sprawling structure would dispute it. The roof area alone covers two and a quarter acres. The present Duke of Roxburghe, whose family, the Innes-Kers, has lived here since the early 18th century, confirms that a good proportion of the Castle is regularly used and visited by the public, although he and his family occupy only the central block which is two rooms deep. The east wing is the estate office, stables and garage. The west wing provides flats for the staff. "It is," said the Duke, "essentially a family home."

In an age of unemployment these are probably four of the safer small businesses around. The dairyman at work in a perfectly restored setting at Manderston House in Berwickshire is an integral part of Scotland's expanding tourist trade; the blacksmith in celebrated Border hunting country has rarely been busier; the Peeblesshire "monumental mason", as his trade is still called, will never be without a job, for life goes on but it also stops; while the saddler in Aberdeenshire will find employment so long as there are pony-mad children, indulgent parents, and the Horse of the Year Show.

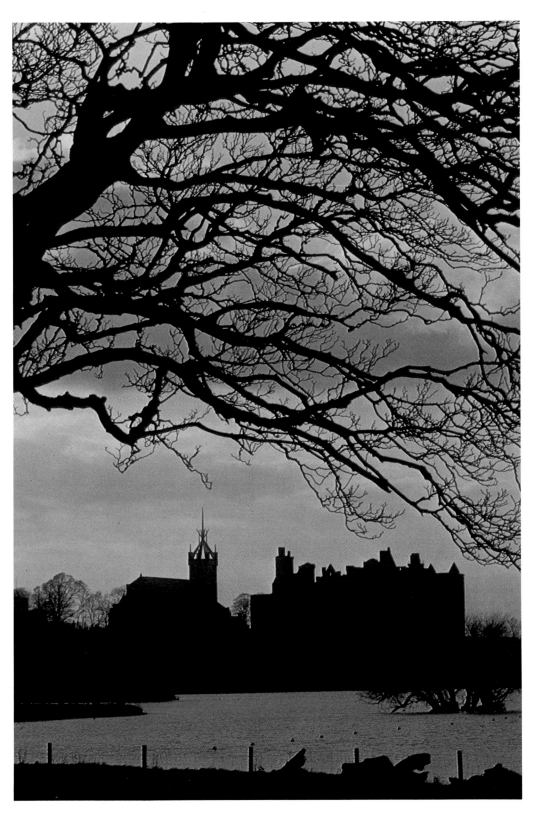

If too many of Scotland's great buildings are hung around with poignant memories, that is because so much of Scotland's history consists of missed opportunities and unnecessary disasters. The ruins of Linlithgow Palace in West Lothian recall the worst of these – the Battle of Flodden in 1513, which was not only a savage defeat but ended the reign of the greatest of Scottish kings, James IV. It was a battle which James had never wished to fight – he was forced into it by his French allies. His death robbed Scotland of a Renaissance monarch. "The reign of James IV was, economically and culturally, the Golden Age of Scottish civilization," wrote Lewis Grassic Gibbon. "Its duration was brief and its fate soon that which had overtaken the Golden Age of the happy Pict hunters three thousand years before. The end of James IV at Flodden plunged the country into 15 years of misgovernment . . ."

"Tantallon has three sides of wall-like rock and one side of rock-like wall," wrote the geologist Hugh Miller, and for three hundred years it was an almost impregnable Douglas stronghold, defended mainly against their arch-enemies, the Northumberland Percys. It was held by the Scots against Cromwell, but surrendered after relentless bombardment by General Monck in 1651, when it was partly destroyed. Today, at a distance, it is one of the most romantic sights in Scotland.

Beyond it, in the Firth of Forth, is an equally formidable, though natural, fortress, the Bass Rock, a prison under the Covenanters, but then, as now, more famous for its bird life. The gannets, or solan geese, which breed here, were once regarded as a delicacy. The *Edinburgh Advertiser* of 5 August 1768 carried a notice: "SOLAN GOOSE. There is to be sold by John Watson Jun. ate his Stand at the Poultry, Edinburgh, all lawful days of the week, wind and weather serving, good and fresh Solan Geese. Any who have occasion for the same may have them at reasonable rates." I doubt if the Royal Society for the Protection of Birds would be amused.

Close up and floodlit, Edinburgh Castle (left) dwarfs and outshines its surroundings. The narrow streets and tall tenements of the Old Town beneath it were so rank and stinking in the 18th century that afterwards visitors could often remember little but the smell. Everyone knows that Edinburgh householders simply tossed their sewage into the gutter with a shouted warning, but it is equally the case that stern laws were brought in to stop the practice, and that if you could prove that you had been unpleasantly soaked and could trace the perpetrator then justice would be done and a heavy fine imposed. The Castle itself was actually responsible for some of the overcrowding beneath its battlements, since in earlier days everyone wanted to build as close to it as possible to benefit from its protection.

Above, Edinburgh Castle seen from the Calton Hill. "Of all places for a view, this Calton Hill is perhaps the best," wrote Robert Louis Stevenson, "since you can see the Castle, which you lose from the Castle, and Arthur's Seat, which you cannot see from Arthur's Seat. It is the place to stroll on one of those days of sunshine and east wind. . . ." It is also a place dotted with a series of neo-classical monuments which once earned Edinburgh the mock title of the Modern Athens.

The most stirring story of the Hill is that of the young Earl of Bothwell who captured, fatally, the attention of Mary Stuart by galloping his horse straight down it in the course of a tournament. "Women born to be controll'd, Stoop to the forward and the bold" was his thesis, and it seems to have worked.

Two faces of the modern soldier: right, a sergeant major in the Argyll and Sutherland Highlanders at Edinburgh Castle; below, the Atholl Highlanders on parade.

Anyone who has served in uniform will recognize with a chill that combination of raw discipline and unbridled sarcasm which is the unique feature of the sergeant major. This one has spotted something not to his liking, and there is every likelihood that the next man to cross his path is in for a withering offensive.

The kindly sergeant hurrying forward to help one of his men forming up for a parade is very different. These are more your amateur soldiers, and there is a distinct touch of the Dad's Army about the Atholl Highlanders, the only private army in Britain. They wear the juniper sprig which is the badge of the Murrays of Atholl, but they would perhaps look a little smarter if the Duke could provide them with identical shoes.

It is, of course, the height of impertinence to place these two pictures together. On the left is an example of pure Scottish kitsch – the minikilts, the puffed sleeves, the cheeky doublets worn by these girls are a mere parody of pomp and circumstance. On the other hand, the grave gentlemen taking part in the annual Kirking the Council ceremony in Edinburgh, with their scarlet cloaks and their fore-and-aft hats, and their goldtopped batons, command our instant respect. Well, perhaps there is something marginally absurd about the one in the kilt, and the ushers look a trifle embarrassed, but there is no *real* comparison . . . is there?

Edinburgh waitresses (this one is serving wine at Prestonfield House on the outskirts of the city) take a keen and interventionist line at the table. "You'll not be wanting the *whole* bottle," I was instructed by one in Queen Street. "I wouldn't have that," I was ordered by another, "It's a terrible price to pay."

A winter scene in the Queen's Park, Edinburgh, looking towards Salisbury Crags. "A' the hills are covered wi' snaw, and Winter's noo come fairly!" was the song the children used to sing when snow appeared, according to Robert Louis Stevenson. More recently, the citizens of Edinburgh were thrown into a tizzy when the Queen complained about the untidiness in Holyrood Park. A clean-up was organized, but one indignant reader of *The Scotsman* wrote: "There are many square miles of midden surrounding the Queen's London home; perhaps she should turn her attention to them. . . ."

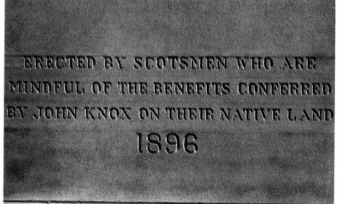

ERECTED BY SCOTSMEN WHO ARE
MINDFUL OF THE BENEFITS CONFERRED
BY JOHN KNOX ON THEIR NATIVE LAND
1896

George Heriot's School, with Edinburgh Castle in the background. If the playground of this famous school looks a little like a military parade ground, that may be because it was founded on the stern Scotch principles of firm discipline and high academic standards. Its founder was known as Jingling Geordie, and his tombstone explains why: "Goldsmith, Burgess of Edinburgh, and sometime jeweller to King James the Sixth". As well as being favoured by royalty, he was wealthy, leaving over £23,000 for the foundation of George Heriot's Hospital, for the "maintenance, relief, bringing up and education of orphans". Nowadays the orphans have been replaced by the children of the well-heeled middle class.

Note the sprinkling of girls on the playground. They were first admitted in 1979.

Another benefactor who made his money by catering for the tastes of the Edinburgh wealthy. James Gillespie, "tobacco and snuff manufacturer", left £12,000 to found a hospital for old people and £2,700 to start a school. The hospital was closed in 1870, but the school carried on and is now a comprehensive. Amongst its more celebrated former pupils is Miss Muriel Spark who immortalized it in *The Prime of Miss Jean Brodie.*

"Cities like Edinburgh seem so permanent that we grow fiercely indignant over the pointless destruction of a few fine buildings at the hands of old-fashioned philistines," wrote George Scott-Moncrieff in his excellent study of Edinburgh. And he waxed particularly indignant over the "restoration" of Lady Stair's Close (left), which he judged to have been refaced by "an architect who must have heartily despised the work of his predecessor". But the Close, and many others like it in Edinburgh's Old Town, are still rich in atmosphere.

Charlotte Square (right), which epitomizes the Augustan Age of Edinburgh's architecture, has been called the wealthiest acre in Britain because it now houses the offices of many of the companies involved in North Sea oil exploitation, as well as the more traditional solicitors' offices where the deeds of Scotland's great estates are held.

What can one say of the marvels of the New Town except that they matched the spirit of the times. "Self-conscious no doubt," wrote Scott-Moncrieff, "but self-confident forbye. . . ."

The one thing Edinburgh does not have in its midst is a great river. Instead it has the Water of Leith – this view looks across it to Leith itself. It is sometimes referred to disrespectfully as the Puddocky Burn, but in the old days it was one of the busiest stretches of water in Britain – along less than twenty miles there were no fewer than seventy mills. These days its tasks are less demanding: it looks pretty in a sunset and carries much unwanted drainage out to the harbour of Leith.

Normally, the crossing of the Forth Bridge by train is an anticlimax. Dwarfed by the confusion of tubed pillars, one gets no idea of the monstrous shape of the thing. But as Douglas Corrance found when he crossed on the old railway engine, Maud, to take this picture from the footplate, there is nothing like doing it under steam. "It was an exhilarating trip," he reports. "You get a proper feel for the bridge."

The man emerging from the freezing waters of the Forth is Bill Stein, the oldest handicapped person to have swum the English Channel, for whom crossing the Forth was only a warm-up. He cannot move his neck, therefore he wears a snorkel.

The last picture shows the two Bridges moving side by side into the low-lying cloud over South Queensferry. The Rail Bridge plods across like an ancient dinosaur. The Road Bridge swoops in one swift plunge like the darting neck of a swan.

Across the River Forth from Edinburgh, restoration, Victorian style: Dunfermline Abbey's rebuilt tower proclaiming King Robert the Bruce in stone letters round a turreted parapet is not an improvement in the best of taste. The original building was first improved in the 11th century by Malcolm Canmore who imported Romanesque designs from England. But most of them were dismantled by John Knox's zealous reformers, and although there are remains of Malcolm's palace inside, what we see now is largely 19th century. Both Malcolm and his wife Margaret, who died of grief on hearing of his death, are buried here, along with fourteen other kings and queens.

This milestone in Fife shows precisely where we are: "Newport 0", it proclaims.

Falkland Palace in Fife carries a rather more modest contribution to the art of beautification. The inscription on this stone plaque is dedicated to "IR6" – James VI – and the wording shows it was carved by a man who knew which side his bread was buttered – unlike Bishop Andrew Melville who stood up at Falkland Palace and called James "God's silly vassal" for opposing Melville's reforms. Falkland was the great courtyard palace of the Stuarts, an early example of the French Renaissance style, and a symbol of the Auld Alliance between Scotland and France.

Alexander Selkirk, on whom Daniel Defoe is said to have based *Robinson Crusoe*, was a native of Largo in Fife. He was clearly a troublemaker who got into scrapes at home then joined the South Seas buccaneers at the age of 28. In 1704 he got into a bigger scrape by quarrelling with his captain and being put ashore on the island of Juan Fernandez. He lived there for four years and four months, then was rescued and returned to Largo where he died in 1721, having meanwhile joined the navy proper and become a lieutenant. The statue is in Lower Largo. He is, of course, dressed like Robinson Crusoe.

Culross, in Fife, where these schoolchildren are enthusiastically noting the improvements and even the dustman stands proudly outside the renovated electricity sub-station, was once a seaport and coaling station on the River Forth. Then, as both industries declined, so it decayed. It was taken in hand by the National Trust for Scotland and has been painstakingly restored. "Even the electricity board entered into the spirit of this enterprise," says *The Shell Guide to Scotland*, "and no one would suspect that one of the visibly and genuinely old houses actually contains an electricity sub-station." Douglas Corrance was particularly pleased by the composition of his pyramid of schoolchildren, each looking in a different direction.

Crail, with its protective little harbour, was once known for modest catches of lobster, crab, salt herrings and Crail capons (smoked haddock). Now even those are not easy to come by. No longer a regular fishing base, the harbour is now a place for pleasure boats – a centre for strictly amateur sea-fishing trips.

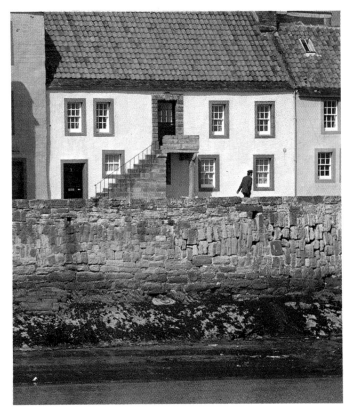

The East Neuk of Fife is one of the minor miracles of the Scottish coastline. Each one of its little harbour villages seems to outdo the last in charm and style. On the right is St Monans, with a distinctive Fife fisherman's house whose outside stair leads from the first floor to the ground. The ground floor tends to be the functional one with kitchen, storerooms, etc.; the first floor is posher – for guests.

Anstruther (below) is perhaps the "capital" of the East Neuk, with a fishing museum at the harbourhead and another on the floating North Carr lightship. But museums these days are almost more numerous than fishing boats. The only Fife port now with its own regular fishing fleet is Pittenweem, which has been saved by the national appetite for scampi – or nephrop as it is locally and unromantically known. There they have about sixty boats regularly in the harbour. Here there are likely to be no more than half a dozen.

It is something of a tradition in St Andrews, on the North Fife coast, to walk down to the end of the sturdy little pier, above, inspect the deep clear sea water at the end of it, then walk back again, pondering the great issues of the day. Among the strollers are students of the University, Scotland's oldest, in their distinctive scarlet cloaks.

Nearby, the remains of the Cathedral confront one with the image of John Knox, who came back to Scotland after a long exile in England and on the Continent to begin his stern work of reform. Amongst his early tasks was an assault on the Cathedral here. His followers dismantled it, and the task of destruction was completed later under Oliver Cromwell.

Lewis Grassic Gibbon blamed Knox's reputation entirely on his supporters. "Knox himself was of heroic mould," he wrote. "Had his followers, far less his allies, been of like mettle, the history of Scotland might have been strangely and splendidly different." As for the object of so much of Knox's vitriol, Mary Queen of Scots, she had "the face, mind, manners and morals of a well-intentioned but hysterical poodle".

41

Driving off from the first tee outside the Royal and Ancient clubhouse at St Andrews, it is hard to tell from the joyless expression on the golfer's face whether he has struck well or struck less well. Golf is still, in Scotland, a more democratic sport than anywhere else in the world – even here where it was nurtured. Why, then, has Scotland not produced more champions? Not since the Morrises, father and son, have the Scots truly dominated the rest of the world. Old Tom was the greatest golfer in the world until 1868 when his son Tommy won the Open Championship, held the title for the next five years, then drank himself to death after the tragic death of his wife and unborn child.

From below. the solid foundations of the Tay Road Bridge stretching across the Firth of Tay should reinforce the impression of Dundee as a stable old-fashioned Victorian town, with factory chimneys, civic buildings, churches and houses built to last. But, with an unemployment rate of 20 per cent, the city faces as difficult a future as many other big towns where the recession has bitten deep. While Aberdeen has cornered the oil boom and expanded, Dundee is running hard to stand still. But it is still a place of great energy; it has adapted to the new electronics industry; it is the capital of Tayside Region; it has a good university and an excellent theatre; and it is rightly famous for having the most beautiful girls in Scotland.

A glamorous Dundee, seen through the filigree of an elegant drinking fountain on the south shore of the Firth of Tay. Dundee is not really like that. It is still a manufacturing town, although the old industries, like jute, have long been replaced. Fifty years ago, bemoaning Dundee's economic decline, Hugh MacDiarmid wrote, "Dundee is dust; And Aberdeen a shell..." which prompted a Dundee paper to demand (not surprisingly) what MacDiarmid meant by being "so damnably elliptical". What he meant was that greedy capitalists had sucked Dundee dry and cast it aside. But he was a bit premature. Dundee has turned to more modern industries, and, in new hands, even the old jam trade has been saved.

On the terraces at Dens Road, home of Dundee Football Club. The shot is a little unfair. It looks a bit like a prison camp, suggesting that violence amongst the fans is an ever-present problem. Not so: despite the fact that Dundee is traditionally Protestant supported, while its rival, Dundee United, is Catholic, relations between the two are reasonably good, and trouble is minimal.

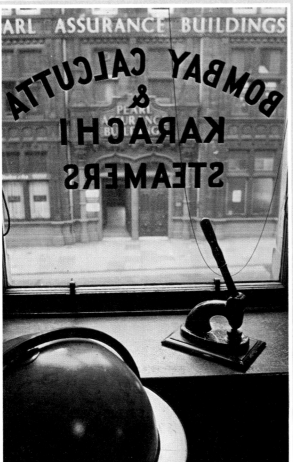

The offices of D.C. Thomson, who own the *Dundee Courier* as well as a whole string of children's comics like the *Beano* and the *Dandy*. They look as old-fashioned as the attitude of the firm itself. Modern trends, like the encroachment of the trade union movement and the prying of outside journalists, are sternly repudiated.

The big Pearl Assurance building, seen through the window of an old-established steamship company, harks back to the days of Dundee's rich trading past when confidence in the future was taken for granted, and words like recession and unemployment were not part of the vocabulary.

We are in Murray country, and above is Blair Castle in Perthshire, seat of the Murray family who have been Earls and Dukes of Atholl since the 16th century. There has been a castle here since 1269, although the present white gleaming structure dates mainly from the 18th century. The Castle and its estates say something of the permanency of Scottish land tenure. In 1874 the Atholl estates covered 194,600 acres. In 1970 they still ran to 130,000 acres. Inside the Castle are some of the mementoes of a rich and turbulent past, and Blair has become a magnet for streams of visiting tourists. It is also something of a centre for activities ranging from piping competitions to horse trials. The present Duke lives in one wing of the building. "I think if one had to live in the whole Castle it would probably be somewhat cold in the winter," he commented. ". . . Also, it would be almost impossible ever to get a hot meal."

Take a close look at this shot on the right of Gleneagles Golf Course, also in Perthshire and one of the world's most famous. That golfer in the Sam Snead hat might be tapping in his putt anywhere from Singapore to San Sebastian. But there in the background is an unmistakeable figure: the Scottish caddy. The cap, the suit and the brown brogues make no concession to modern styles.

There have been caddies around since the 18th century, although, they were originally called "fore-caddies", people who went ahead to see where the ball fell. At St Andrews, in June 1771, it was laid down that caddies would get "fourpence for going the length of the hole, known as the Hole of the Cross, and if they go further than that hole, they are to get sixpence – and no more". That at least has changed.

Rannoch Moor, on the border of Argyll and Perthshire, is a strange and desolate place, empty, blasted and unreal. Legends surround it, and it acted as a protection to the Glencoe MacDonalds in their mountain fastness farther north, perhaps because rival clans were reluctant to venture across it.

The "little houses" of Dunkeld in central Perthshire, seen from the fountain in the centre of The Cross, Dunkeld. These 18th-century dwellings were, after the Second World War, a slum. There was even a proposal to pull them down altogether. Then much of the property was given to the National Trust for Scotland which joined with the local council to restore them. The result is one of the most perfectly preserved town centres in Scotland, with a layout which still conforms to its early medieval shape.

Perth has an air of ill-concealed prosperity, with broad streets and neo-classical porticoes overlooking the sweep of the Tay. There is little to remind one of its violent past, when Robert the Bruce recaptured it from the English by wading the river, or when Clans Chattan and Kay staged a battle on what is now the North Inch, or when John Knox, "vehement against idolatry", preached his most famous sermon, provoking a riot in which St John's Church was sacked. But the bells were saved, and I once heard them playing old Scottish tunes. If Knox would have called it idolatry, I do not know, but the tourists liked it.

An antiques shop as it should be, in Strathyre, Perthshire. The antiques business in Scotland (as elsewhere) has expanded enormously, in step with tourism and the desire of property owners to exchange some of their property for money. The great charm and attraction of the business for amateur collectors is the possibility of picking up (or disposing of) a bargain. But beware: it can be a cut-throat trade despite its apparent gentility, where prices are determined as much by the likely gullibility of the customer as by the intrinsic value of the article in question.

The grave of Rob Roy MacGregor at Balquhidder in eastern Perthshire (top left). He was a rogue, convict, bandit, double-dealer, but clearly a man of enormous magnetism who raised two hundred of his widely dispersed clan to the Jacobite standard in 1715, despite the fact that he was not even the chief. But he appears thereafter to have acted as a government spy for the Duke of Argyll who then turned him over to the law. Imprisoned, almost transported to Barbados, he was reprieved and returned home to Balquhidder where he died gracefully of old age. Red-haired, with tree-trunk legs, he was said to have had arms so long he could tie the garters of his hose two inches below the knee without having to bend down.

The study of old tombstones is endlessly fascinating. Their symbols and images are open to wide interpretation. But the tombstone at Innerpeffray near Crieff (top right) is interesting mainly because it is so un-Scottish. The face dominating it looks as if it might have come from Easter Island rather than Crieff. The Coupar Angus stone (bottom right) carries all the more obvious symbols of death and, above, the winged soul fluttering upwards to heaven. It is characteristic that the Montrose gravestone (bottom left) should carry a ship – it is a seafaring town, and the grave is therefore that of a mariner.

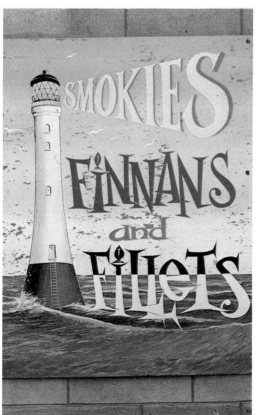

Despite the collapse of the Scottish fishing industry, Arbroath on the Angus coast still has a busy harbour where up to fifty boats bustle in daily to unload their cargo of scampi and white fish – which include, of course, the haddock to be turned into the local and justly famous delicacy, Arbroath smokies, in little kiln sheds nearby. At first glance these boats may look delightfully old-fashioned, but note the radar, the sonar, the echo sounders, and all the other paraphernalia which these days are part of the essential equipment of the modern fisherman.

The Arbroath pageant, held yearly in the ruins of the town's Abbey, commemorates the Declaration of Arbroath in 1320, which first enunciated the principle of Scottish independence. It was addressed to the Pope, and though there is not much evidence that he paid a great deal of attention to it, its resounding phrases still excite: "We fight, not for glory, nor riches, nor honour, but only for that liberty which no true man relinquishes but with his life".

Autumn beech trees – tall, golden and luminous – on Deeside, Aberdeenshire. Both rivers, the Don and the Dee, have their admirers: "A mile o' Don's worth twa o' Dee Except for salmon, stone and tree" goes one old rhyme, while another says:
"Bluidthirsty Dee
Each year taks three,
But bonny Don
Asks for none."
But Queen Victoria rendered the competition uneven when she chose Balmoral as her Highland home, and Deeside became "Royal". There is no doubt that she doted on it. "Here," wrote Lytton Strachey, "her happiest days passed. In after years, when she looked back on them, a kind of glory, a radiance as of an unearthly holiness, seemed to glow about those golden hours." My own favourite remark of Queen Victoria's concerns the people: "We were always in the habit of conversing with the Highlanders," she noted in her journal, "with whom one comes so much in contact in the Highlands."

TO COMMEMORATE
HUGH MACDIARMID
(CHRISTOPHER MURRAY GRIEVE)
POET, PATRIOT, MAN OF LETTERS, COUNCILLOR, JOURNALIST
ON THE "MONTROSE REVIEW" AT THIS SITE, 1919-1929.
ERECTED BY THE MONTROSE SOCIETY   FEBRUARY 1982

Montrose, north of Arbroath, seen here across a beached oil rig, a reminder of its new-found importance to the North Sea oil business. It is a comely red-sandstone east coast town – but it is not without pretension. In the late 18th century it attracted the gentry and the nobility for the winter season: it built schools for their children and assembly rooms for their entertainment. It was, said a local minister at the time, "more distinguished by the residence of persons of opulence and fashion than of commerce and industry"

But commerce and industry always took precedence over leisure, and trade was with places as far away as St Petersburg, Antwerp and Stockholm. Inside the Parish Church tower is this frieze commemorating the great shipping days of the town, when the big clippers crowded its harbour. If you look closely you will see Victorian graffiti overlaying it, together with some less attractive 20th-century examples.

Hugh MacDiarmid, Scotland's finest modern poet, worked as a cub reporter on the *Montrose Review* through the 1920s, as the great trading days declined. He had a solid training here, but he conceived no great admiration for Scottish journalism. It did not, in his view, show any serious concern with Scottish affairs. "It may be noted," he wrote caustically, "that any papers I quote in relation to Scottish affairs are never the leading Scottish dailies, which have always been and remain utterly untrustworthy on such matters."

Quite suddenly, on the bleak and fearsome stretch of road that runs north from the lushness of Perthshire into the forbidding moorland of the Grampians, one comes across a white village in the middle of nowhere. This is Dalwhinnie, and Douglas Corrance has caught it by surprise, struck by the end of a rainbow, lit by a chance spear of sunlight from a dark and lugubrious sky. But the impending rain is the reason Dalwhinnie is there at all – its distillery turns the pure and fragrant water of the surrounding hills into something darker, every bit as fragrant, but a little different – Scotch whisky. The "pagoda" rooftops of Scottish distilleries were developed to protect the kiln and filter the smoke from it during the delicate stage of drying the grain, a process during which it becomes the "malt".

South of the Dee and in sight of the royal residence at Balmoral rear the sudden cliffs of Lochnagar, which had a more poetical admirer than Queen Victoria. Lord Byron was a local: his mother was a Gordon of Gight. Every now and then his Scottishness came out, not always to the improvement of his poetry:

"England! Thy beauties are tame and domestic
To one who has roved o'er mountains afar;
Oh for the crags that are wild and majestic;
The steep, frowning glories of dark Loch na Garr!"

The Lairig Ghru pass, highest in the
Cairngorm Mountains, seen from
Aviemore station nearby. For
climbers this is a challenging way to
cross into Aberdeenshire. But it can
be treacherous and lives are still
lost in the Cairngorms, at least in
part because of the weather's
daunting unpredictability.

Aviemore's most famous pastime is catering for skiing in the Cairngorms, and despite the uncertainty of the Scottish snow, each year the crowds grow. Now the existing slopes are bursting at the seams. An attempt to open up new ski runs by building a lift and tows on the steep slopes known as Lurcher's Gully failed when conservationists objected to the harm it would do to the natural habitat. So Aviemore cannot expand the only industry it has. On a bad day the queues will be so long that a half hour wait for five minutes of downhill skiing is not uncommon . . .

. . . but on a good day, with the sun shining on fresh snow, the only appropriate comment is "Whaur's your Switzerland noo?"

Shinty, still played widely in the north of Scotland (this game is at Kingussie in Inverness-shire), is a vicious form of hockey where the ball is deliberately hit through the air rather than along the ground (note the lofting angle on the sticks). The wretched player here has just been struck on the temple and is sinking lifeless to the ground. His opponent shows every sign of delight and is leaping forward to take possession. That, as the sports commentators would say, is what shinty is all about.

For some folk in the skiing centre of Aviemore the mysteries of stem christies and langlauf and the merits of silver wax over red are wholly irrelevant. Spring takes care of all that white stuff anyway; the daffodils are out; and the skiers are gone for another year.

In a grand house near Newtonmore, Inverness-shire, a family warms up for one of the many Highland balls that take place through the summer social season and often well beyond it. Very soon they will be dancing Scottish reels with several hundred fellow guests, an activity which will involve them whirling each other around at great speed in a series of intricate patterns to the accompaniment of strange cries emitted at irregular but carefully specified moments. Faces will be flushed, those immaculate shirts will steam with sweat, and before the evening is out, the youngest member of the party will be wondering even more what manner of ritual all his elders are caught up in.

This is another tribal rite. A shooting party prepares to set out from Ardverikie House, Loch Laggan, in pursuit of the fast and elusive grouse. This occasion, too, has obscure rules. The shooters, for instance, are not carrying their guns at this point. It is done for them by the keepers (second and fourth from the left). The generally accepted uniform for the well-dressed shot is the Barbour coat (one, three and seven). The smiles disguise the fact that the grouse is sadly on the decline in most parts of Scotland these days – the horse will not, I think, be needed to carry the dead birds back from the moor.

A wildcat at Kincraig wildlife centre in Inverness-shire hisses its defiance. Fierce, lethal in attack, and quite fearless, the European wildcat (*Felis silvestris*) survives in the Scottish Highlands and scarcely anywhere else. It and its African relation (*Felis libyca*) are the stock from which all our domestic cats have sprung. Even as kittens, however, they are untameable. The call of the wild is too strong.

Do not be taken in by the romantic aspect of Dunottar Castle on its fortress headland just south of Stonehaven. Bloody and terrible deeds were done here. William Wallace, who took it from the English in 1296, set fire to it and roasted alive the soldiers who had fled to its chapel for sanctuary; nearly four hundred years later 167 Covenanters, men, women and children, were starved and suffocated to death in its deep dungeons, an act of barbarism which, unlike the Black Hole of Calcutta, has been quietly forgotten.

Crathes Castle, Aberdeenshire, one of the most elegant and best preserved of the Scottish tower houses, is famous for the painted ceilings which adorn three of its rooms – the Chamber of the Nine Nobles, the Green Lady's Room, and the Chamber of the Nine Muses. This ceiling is in the last, and has figures which include one of the muses (right) and two of the five virtues of Wisdom, Justice, Faith, Hope and Charity, all clothed in fashionable costumes of the time – 1599.

61

Craigievar, Aberdeenshire, is, quite simply, the perfect Scottish castle. It rises clean out of green lawns, seven storeys high, its walls straight and uncluttered, to be crowned by a profusion of turrets, high-pitched roofs, decorative stonework and corbelling. The pattern for these tower castles is 14th century, but the design stayed in favour long after its strictly defensive function had lapsed. Craigievar was built between 1610 and 1624. Within sixty years of its completion, this style of domestic architecture, unique in Europe, was to die out completely and quite suddenly.

"The Thane of Cawdor lives, A prosperous gentleman . . ." noted Macbeth as he contemplated the three witches' predictions, and, by the look of Cawdor Castle, overlooking the Inverness Firth, it was indeed the seat of a powerful laird. But none of the present building existed in the days of the real Macbeth (1040–57), son of Findlaech, Mormaer of Moray, King of Alba, and cousin of Duncan, whom he slew in battle near Elgin after Duncan had encroached on his territory, doubtless with the intention of removing Macbeth from the throne. Macbeth himself was apparently a good king, who ruled for all of seventeen years, considered an indication of great stability in those turbulent days. The present castle, with its trees and gardens, is 17th century, but the central keep dates back to 1454, when the Thane of Cawdor was granted a royal licence to fortify the castle. He had dreamed that he would build a new castle wherever a donkey loaded with a box of gold should stop. The Thane tested out the dream, and when the donkey stopped at a hawthorn tree, built the new castle there. In the depths of the guard-room the hawthorn tree still stands. Parts of the interior of the castle are open to visitors, and there is a relaxing coffee shop off the main courtyard. A spiral staircase connects the tower room to the guard-room with its ancient tree. The Campbells of Cawdor were every bit as acquisitive as most members of that land-hungry clan, and in 1612 bought out one of the last great Chiefs of Clan Donald, Angus of Islay, for a few hundred pounds. But it should be said in their favour that they were one of the few clans to extend the hand of friendship to the much-persecuted MacGregors, against whom a campaign of deliberate genocide was organized in the early 17th century. The Campbells of Cawdor still hold the castle today.

Aberdeen has two universities, which were amalgamated in 1826. King's College (on the right) is the older by a hundred years. Marischal College was first founded, in 1593, because King's was thought to be too old-fashioned and slow in responding to the demands of the Reformation. King's continued to take its time – it was the last university in Scotland to abandon the old system of teaching by regents, who took their own class through every subject, whatever their own specialization. And it was amongst the last to abandon Latin as the basic teaching language.

Marischal College's main building (above) was completed in 1906, and when it was opened it was the second largest granite hall in the world – after the Escorial in Spain.

The granite bishop here is Bishop Elphinstone of Aberdeen, "father" of Scottish education, to whom is attributed the Education Act of 1496 and who was the prime mover in the founding of Aberdeen University. He was an essentially practical man who saw to the importing of wheelbarrows and gunpowder (for quarry blasting) as well as the distributing of "mass-books, manuals, matin-books, and protuus books [breviaries] after our own Scots use", which gave his young students a proper grounding for their lives ahead.

There are occasional coincidences in life which give the photographer cause for rejoicing. Aberdeen is the oil capital of Scotland, the so-called Houston of the North, as the ship in the harbour explains. Then, on top, its radar mast echoes the granite tower of the Salvation Army Citadel which may well outlive the oil.

Aberdeen has become vital to the industry, with eight service and supply stations for the rigs, and the world's largest helicopter airport. But how long will it last? The year 2020 is mentioned as zero date for when the oil will run out. Long before then Aberdeen will have had to diversify to survive.

A thoroughly civilized scene inside Aberdeen's Art Gallery on Schoolhill. The lady reading her *Guardian* in between shopping trips and the gentleman stealing a quick nap are treating the Gallery as it should be – a friendly place to be used as a home from home, with a bit of culture thrown in.

The quality of these roses at Maryculter, near Aberdeen, helps explain why that city has won the Britain in Bloom competition so often it is no longer allowed to take part. There are roses everywhere – dancing down the centres of dual carriageways and enlivening the bleakest of granite streets.

Footdee, by the head of the North Pier in Aberdeen, was formerly spelled "Fittie" or "Futtie" (as it is still pronounced). The modern spelling is an attempt to explain its name in terms of the River Dee, but in fact it is on the Den Burn. Built in the 19th century for the fisherfolk, its cottages are laid out in three squares and are steadily being restored.

The bizarre tap in the form of a human face is a maverick piece of local art in Footdee. Its creator, like those responsible for so much Scottish folklore, is Anon.

Aberdeen fish market was once one of the sights of Britain, with hundreds of tons of deep-sea fish being unloaded daily to be auctioned on the quayside to the accompaniment of great noise, good humour, and an air of general prosperity. These days, Aberdeen, like many other fishing ports, is suffering from a collapse of the industry. In the old days, these skate being sold off to a remarkably uninterested clientele would probably have been thrown back. Aberdeen has even surrendered the distinction of being the largest fishing port in Scotland – that distinction has been won by Peterhead, farther north.

The fishwives and fish lads still don their gutting gear to tackle the fish once they are landed, but what with one thing and another they tend to have more time now to sit around and chat.

Work nears completion on a trawler at a boatyard in Macduff, said to be one of the safest havens for fishing boats on the whole of the Moray Firth. It is a lively place, bustling with activity. The harbour was extended some years ago, with Government help, and the £150,000 investment has paid off handsomely.

Pennan, just south of Macduff, is another fishing village, where the breadwinners are frequently far away, serving on fishing fleets off Iceland, Norway or the west coast. Steep cliffs run all along the coast here; one of the few natural openings is Quayman Cave, once a notorious smugglers' haunt.

The Post Office, Glenlivet. There is a wonderful simplicity about its interior which has been reduced to bare essentials – the bound volumes of the register, the two sacks, the clock, the scales, the calendar and the notices. And, of course, the postmistress, as important for relaying first-class local knowledge as for selling first-class stamps.

Ramsay MacDonald's birthplace, Lossiemouth. MacDonald's reputation has not stood high of late, and reading his own account of the view from this front door one does not automatically warm to his prose: "Away to the north, across the Firth, rose the pale blue hills of Sutherland and Ross; to the south lay the fertile farms of Morayshire sloping up through green wood and purple moorland into the blue tops of the Grampians; to the east swept the sea . . ." and so on.

Duff House in Banff, modelled on the Villa Borghese in Rome, is evidence that even the greatest architects can become involved in the kind of legal squabbles that usually accompany more mundane buildings. Commissioned by the 1st Earl of Fife from William Adam in 1735, it cost £70,000 (a colossal amount by the standards of the day) to build only the central block. Then a crack appeared and the Earl went to law. The quarrel was so bitter that the Earl refused to set foot inside his new house. It has now been restored by the Department of the Environment. There are no cracks to be seen.

North of Newburgh, on the Aberdeenshire coast, stands this gaunt and sprawling ruin. Slains Castle was given to the Earl of Errol by Robert the Bruce in one of his many handouts after the Battle of Bannockburn. But it was blown up by James VI when the 9th Earl rebelled in 1594. He was pardoned and returned to build a new and grander castle, but that too is now reduced to bare walls, giving it a distinctly Transylvanian look – indeed Bram Stoker, the author of *Dracula*, used it as a model for the Count's hideous abode.

This gothic shot is of Ruthven Barracks near Kingussie in Inverness-shire. Once this was a stronghold of Alexander Stewart, fourth son of Robert II and known as the Wolf of Badenoch. But the ruins here are of the Barracks built in 1718 and defended in 1746 by one Sergeant Molloy and fourteen men against the Jacobites who finally burnt it to prevent its further use.

Fort George, another barracks, on the Moray Firth, was begun in the aftermath of the Forty-Five. It has a fine architectural pedigree. One of the contractors was William Adam, and although he died before work began, his son John was responsible for all the masonwork and brickwork. It is still used as a barracks. I can testify that it is a cold place in which to parade in a kilt.

This charming little church at Daviot in Inverness-shire used to stand on a peninsula within a loop of the A9 as it headed towards Inverness, giving the motorist a chance to observe and enjoy it from virtually every angle as he passed. Now the road has been straightened out, and it is seen only briefly and from a distance. But it is well worth stopping for a closer look.

Castle Urquhart, on the north side of Loch Ness, is a splendid ruin, poised on a bluff overlooking the water. It was destroyed in 1692, the year of the Glencoe massacre, to prevent its occupation by the Jacobites.

Loch Ness has no need of any underwater creature, mythical or otherwise, to excite the imagination. It is long, deep and dark. The rumours of its strange qualities go back to St Columba's time, but the most extraordinary episode in its history took place on 1 November 1755 at the same time as the Lisbon earthquake, when the loch, which goes down to one thousand feet in places, was shaken by underground reverberations and assumed a life of its own. It began to ebb and flow, and one three-foot-high tidal wave ran the whole of its length, on up the River Oich, and flooded the shores for thirty feet.

Little wonder that stories of a monstrous presence somewhere beneath the surface have been given such currency.

Inverness with its Castle and the River Ness behind, and, in front, an old observatory ready to be converted for someone with a taste for eccentric accommodation and a bird's-eye view. Inverness is traditionally the capital of the Highlands, but those who reckon the Highlands only truly begin north of the Caledonian Canal see it more as a gateway. Indeed, there is evidence that the inhabitants thought of it as separate. Captain Edward Burt, who travelled through the Highlands in the 18th century, noted that the distinction then was one of language. "The natives [of Inverness] do not call themselves Highlanders," he wrote. "Not so much on account of their low situation, as because they speak English."

This suspension bridge across the Ness was built after the stone bridge which once stood here was swept away in the great flood of 1849. Ness bridges have had a chequered history, with at least one other disaster when a wooden bridge collapsed in 1663 with two hundred men, women and children on it. But, as everyone in Inverness knows, the real disaster occurred when there were too many bridges. The Brahan Seer, that great Highland prophet, predicted in the 17th century that there would be a worldwide tragedy if ever it were possible to cross the Ness dry shod at five places. A fifth bridge was put up temporarily in August 1939. Next month Hitler marched into Poland. . . .

Sunset over the Black Isle, Ross-shire, which is neither black nor an island, but a broad peninsula running northeast from Inverness and marking the southern flank of the Cromarty Firth. At the mouth of the Firth it plunges into the sea in steep red-sandstone cliffs which now overlook the oil-platform construction yard at Nigg. The oil industry brought a few years of frenetic activity and much local employment to the area during building. Now the workforce tends to be specialized and from outside, and local unemployment has crept up again. But those who predicted the destruction of wildlife in the area during the short boom have been proved wrong. A wide variety of wildfowl still breeds on the mud flats of Nigg Bay.

The Black Isle Show marks a high point of the year, with fierce competition among local farmers for the "best in show" prizes. The cattle these days are often of foreign breed, unlike this Highland cow and her calf; but the farmers are good Ross-shire stock and hardly seem to alter, year in, year out.

"A Sunday in Scotland is, for the traveller, like a thunderstorm at a picnic. You get wet, you can't go on, and all your good humour vanishes." Thus moaned Theodor Fontane in his 19th-century letters from Scotland. The reason is, of course, that every decent soul was in the kirk, listening to long sermons and even longer *ex tempore* prayers. This church interior in Cromarty and the well-thumbed hymn books immediately evoke the wheezing harmonium, the singsong psalms and the lady in the third pew who thinks she has "a voice". All this, complained Lewis Grassic Gibbon, is "as fantastically irrelevant to contemporary Scottish affairs as the appendix is to the human body". But he did add that there was something to be said for "the blessed peace and ease of two hours' rest in the pews".

This is in the nature of a little episcopal joke. The minister at Rescobie Church in Angus, you see, is unique. As the sign outside indicates, he is the only Bishop in the Church of Scotland. Get it?

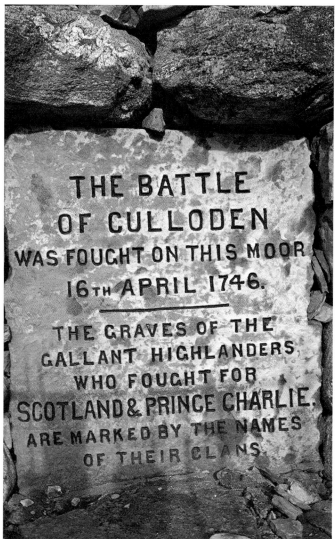

This stone at Fortrose on the Black Isle marks the 17th-century Brahan Seer whose prophecies are held to have been remarkably accurate. Too accurate for his own good. He is said to have been burned in tar by an outraged Countess of Seaforth after he had "seen" her husband's unfaithfulness. Just before his death he predicted the end of the Seaforth line, which duly came about, but not all his prophecies materialized. Even his "archivist", Alexander Mackenzie, who investigated all his sayings, referred to his own research as "a slight palliative for obtruding such nonsense on the public".

The plaque commemorating the Battle of Culloden in April 1746. There are almost as many myths about it as about the Brahan Seer, but the current controversy concerns the number of Scots who fought *against* Prince Charlie. There was a fair number of them: the record shows at least four Scottish regiments on Cumberland's strength. But the greatest myths still hang around the Prince and his conduct. It was not thought well of at the time. "There you go for a damned cowardly Italian," said Lord Elcho as the Prince was led from the field in tears to face eventual exile in Rome.

Dunrobin Castle, the seat of the Dukes of Sutherland outside Golspie, is a superb and unexpected sight. As you round a bend on the road south, the sun will, if you are lucky, catch the white walls of a turreted, fairy-tale castle. Closer to, the gardens laid out beneath are as carefully tended as the building itself. The most notable work on the Castle was by Sir Charles Barry, architect of the Houses of Parliament. But it was further renovated by Sir Robert Lorimer after a fire during the First World War when it was used as a hospital.

On the winding road up through Sutherland, just south of Dunrobin, you will pass through Golspie, an attractive little town of brown sandstone, where service, as you can see, comes with a smile and an old-fashioned bicycle. On top of Ben Vraggie, inland from the town, stands a vast memorial to the 1st Duke of Sutherland who counted himself a benefactor to the Highlands but whose handling of the Clearances has meant instead that he is remembered for anything but charity.

Farther north, on the road that wheels and turns along the Caithness coast, there is this house near the delightfully named village of Latheronwheel. Its owner has carefully clipped the ivy on his wall into the shape of a heart, thus showing an aesthetic sense typical of Caithness people.

That Caithness sense for shape and colour is further demonstrated by the Mondrian-like artwork on this boat in Scrabster harbour, where you take the ferry to Orkney. The strong red and blue, and the black-on-white background are only marginally upset by the tea-box lid taped to the wheelhouse.

This is Stromness, hence the Scandinavian look to the building and to the boat with the graceful lines of a proper Orkney craft, square-ended at the stern (Shetland boats are pointed at both ends, being direct descendants of the Viking longships). Stromness is built down to and into the sea. Eric Linklater described it thus: "It meanders, it straggles, in a single narrow street under the steep shelter of Binkie's Brae that guards it against westerly gales, and on its seaward side many of its houses thrust their gables into the bay, and instead of domestic gardens have the privilege of a small pier or jetty. It has one foot in the sea, and all the traffic of its harbour enlivens the windows of its favoured half."

The *other* London airport is on Eday, one of the North Isles of Orkney. The name comes from *lund*, the Norse word for a grove of trees, hence, in pagan terms, possibly a place of culture. Many of the Orkney isles are now linked by the small and versatile Islander aircraft, offering a service which includes the shortest air trip in Britain – one and a half minutes from Westray to its neighbour, Papa Westray.

What looks like the spacious interior of a church is in fact the tiny Italian Chapel on the Orkney island of Lamb Holm, created out of a Nissen hut by Italian prisoners of war who, during the Second World War, worked on the building of the Churchill Barriers – the concrete bulwarks which sealed the eastern entrances to Scapa Flow. After the War, when the chapel began to deteriorate, the men who had made it were traced and invited back to restore their handiwork. Thus its colours today are as bright as those of a Tuscan capella – an improbable sight on the chilly slopes of Lamb Holm.

Off St Magnus Bay in Shetland the ghostly shapes of the Drongs rear up from a silver sea. In a mist these stone fangs can look as sinister as their name. And when the wind gets up they become, in Shelley's words, like islands which "lost in stormy visions, keep with phantoms an unprofitable strife".

The Shetland festival of
Up-Helly-Aa, on the last Tuesday in
January, reaches its climax as a
Viking ship which has been
escorted through the town in a long
and elaborate procession is burnt
at sea. There follows a night of
drinking and dancing, but relatively
little rowdiness under the strict eye
of the Guizer Jarl who is in charge of
proceedings. "Up-Helly-Aa is a
living festival," wrote Eric Linklater,
"and its overt romanticism flows
naturally from a small and secret
spring in the strange heart of
Shetland."

Lerwick goes about its daily
business, reflected in the red blind
of a shop on the main street.

Winter scene in Lerwick harbour. The capital of the Shetlands plays host to fishing vessels from all round the North Sea, including Russia, although not quite as many as in the 16th century during the "Great Fishery" when up to two thousand Dutch "busses", or fishing boats of 80 tons or more, crowded in Bressay Sound, protected by armed men-of-war. The arrival of the oil industry has not spoiled the town whose character still lies in the narrow paved streets which open suddenly now and again on to a lively jostling harbour.

In the hills of South Uist in the Outer Hebrides, Douglas Corrance came face to face with this monarch of the glen and snapped off the kind of shot a photographer can wait a lifetime for. It's a full-grown red stag with a ten-point set of antlers. Even Landseer would have been pleased.

The "black houses" of Lewis, with their fires in the centre of the room and their thatched roofs pitch-dark with soot, were once a familiar feature of the island. Today there are few to see, and most are in a more advanced state of ruin than this one. But they were carefully designed, and you can see the characteristic ledge along the top of the wall, built so that the thatch lay inside it and did not project to catch the wind.

The stones of Callanish in Lewis, like the Ring of Brodgar in Orkney, go back at least two thousand years before Christ, yet their formation is like that of a Celtic cross. They were erected by a people who had studied astronomy but about whom we know virtually nothing. It is this that makes Callanish a place of awe, speculation, and mystery.

A neat and well-ordered crofting community in Lewis. The cutting, turning and transportation of peat, seen in the foreground, is still an important part of community life. "Crofting communities are no more idyllic than any others," noted Dr Alastair Fraser who has studied them, "but like all long-standing human societies, they have a quality absent from newer, larger aggregations. It seems clear that the sense of belonging, of identity, satisfies a fundamental human need."

To a Lewis man, the islands of Uist – North and South – and Benbecula are "the southern isles", lighter and more colourful than his own. Here, Uist swans on still water look like flamingoes on an African lake. Along the shore, the machars, or grassland, is almost tropically bright in summer with wild flowers.

The Harris Tweed industry flourishes, though its products are usually sold in grander places than this shop in Tarbert, Harris. The skills and traditions of weaving and dyeing the tweed go back a long time, but surely the earliest reference is in a curious tale told by Martin Martin in 1695. He heard of a Dutchman, forced by a storm to land at Borera, who walked into a house where he found ten women, their arms and legs stripped bare, flailing away at a piece of cloth. The Dutchman assumed he had walked into a madhouse, but was assured that this was the way the cloth was thickened, or "waulked". "He was convinced," wrote Martin, "though surprised at the manner of it".

We are on Barra, in Compton Mackenzie country. Mackenzie has been accused of caricaturing the islanders in his novels, but he was greatly loved by them. At his funeral, one, Calum Johnston, at the age of 82, played a pipe lament, then died himself, having done this last service for his friend.

An immaculately preserved croft house on South Uist. Note the ropes holding down the thatch. On older houses these would often be weighted by stones. And inside, the smoke from the fire would find its way out through the thatch. But this lady looks as if she has a good sensible Aga in her kitchen.

91

Castlebay on the island of Barra, with the great MacNeil stronghold of Kishmul Castle standing on its promontory. Parts of the Castle date back to the 11th century, but it was badly damaged by fire in the 18th century. Finally, it was repurchased in 1937 by the 45th clan chief, a MacNeil who was also conveniently an American architect. He set about restoring it, and work was completed in 1970. It is the largest ancient monument in the Western Isles.

The plane that takes you to Barra lands on the only runway in Britain which is under water at full tide. The exchanges between pilot and control tower can be a little unorthodox as well, ranging from discussions about the quality of the runway to the availability of groceries.

Altnacealgach – a long name for a small place in Sutherland – means "stream of the cheats", according to local legend, and reflects a tug of war that took place between Sutherland and Ross-shire for this excellent fishing spot.

The view from Stac Polly in Sutherland. The hill on the right is Cul Beag, the one in the centre Cul Mor, "the big hill-back". The latter is a fine peak, 2,786 feet high and well worth climbing although not a "Munro" – those hills over 3,000 feet high, collected by climbers as other people collect stamps.

The gardens at Inverewe are one of the wonders of the west coast of Scotland and testimony to the mildness of the climate. They were planted by an extraordinary man called Osgood Mackenzie, who succeeded by trial and error in making a semi-tropical garden grow and flourish. Mackenzie wrote a book called A Hundred Years in the Highlands, which recorded how he did it, as well as describing his equally single-minded slaughter of any wildlife that moved. "What a big pile it would make if all the black-game I shot here between 1855 and 1900 were gathered into one heap," he wrote. "Now, alas! there is none, and why, who can tell?"

The stones of Gruinard Bay in Wester Ross are a dazzling mixture of quartzite, red sandstone and hard unyielding gneiss, whose colours range from ochre and brown to sea-green and shimmering white, merging into the blue and grey of the sea.

A desolate and deserted croft house of corrugated iron near Inverpolly, Sutherland. Hardly a thing of beauty, its lifespan has been barely half a century. But the inexorable economics that led to the decline of the crofts goes back to before the Clearances, and despite the Crofters Act of 1886 which gave security of tenure, the drift away from the Highlands has continued in fits and starts ever since.

Suilven in Sutherland is the most spectacular of all the strange, isolated "sugar-loaf" peaks of the far northwest of Scotland. It was named by the Vikings who saw it from this angle as they approached it from the sea, and called it *Sul-fjall*, the Pillar Mountain. In fact it is an elongated ridge, one and a half miles long, of which they could see only the western end.

Loch Bad a' Ghaill in Wester Ross with smoke-like cloud pluming from the horizon, looking east towards Beinn an Eoin – the Hill o the Bird. We are in the region of Coigach – the "fifth part" of an area It was originally part of the Cromarties, now lost in the newly designated Highland Region.

Ullapool, in Wester Ross, snaking out on its promontory into Loch Broom, with the sun catching briefly a thin veil of rain. It is a prosperous place. The herring have gone, but now mackerel are big business, with up to forty Eastern European factory ships standing offshore to buy some 150,000 tons during the season. But just as the herring were fished to destruction, so the mackerel are bound to go too, unless strict limits are fixed.

A welcome telephone box on Loch Glendhu in Sutherland – inspiration perhaps for the film *Local Hero*, set in just such an isolated Highland spot.

Achiltibuie, round the coast from Ullapool, was once the village of bachelors, where not one woman of eligible age was to be found, and it used to be a sad place as a consequence. All that has changed now. Amongst the pleasures of the place (apart from the name) is the Summer Isles Hotel, famous for its cooking.

The post office was built around the turn of the century. The postman originally took the mail on foot along a rough coastal track under Ben More Coigach. His wage was 4/6d a week. Today there is a postbus service, but still run by private enterprise.

In Wester Ross a local shepherd and his dog relax briefly before returning to their flock. But all is not quite as it seems. The shepherd, who looks very much at one with his background, is in fact a former Liverpool art student, the kind of contradiction you come across these days in the Highlands, where bearded old crofters often turn out to be retired stockbrokers from Virginia Water.

Loch Shieldaig, with *memento mori* in the foreground. Shieldaig must be the only Scottish loch with an "adopted" island on it. In 1974, Mr and Mrs Armistead Peter III, of Washington D.C., adopted the island and contributed to the National Trust for Scotland's Coastline and Islands Fund the full equivalent of its purchase price.

From Ardachdail in Wester Ross the
Summer Isles recede into yet
another west coast sunset. Now
sparsely populated (one of them
plays host to a herd of wild goats),
the islands were once the target for
an ambitious regeneration plan.
But the western Highlands do not
take eagerly to such ideas, and it
faded into oblivion.

Ruined and remote, Ardvreck Castle
stands reflected in Loch Assynt,
Sutherland. The seat of the
MacLeods of Assynt, it was built in
1597, and it was here that James
Graham, Marquess of Montrose,
poet and warrior, was betrayed to
the Covenanters after his defeat at
the Battle of Carbisdale on 27 April
1650. Within a month he had been
hanged in Edinburgh.

His betrayer did not entirely
benefit from this act of treachery.
Instead of the £20,000 blood money
which the 11th Chief, Neil MacLeod,
expected to receive, he was fobbed
off by Cromwell's government with
a quantity of sour meal, and
Ardvreck was seized by the
MacKenzies in retaliation for his
gross breach of Highland
hospitality.

This is Liathach (pronounced Leargash) – "the grey one" – in the Torridon range in Wester Ross, described by the venerable mountaineer Bill Poucher as "the mightiest and most imposing mountain in Britain". You can almost feel the lacerations where the glaciers have inched their way along its flanks. It has a spectacular cap of white quartzite which, from a distance, can be mistaken for snow, and it offers one of the finest, airiest, and also most hair-raising ridge walks in mainland Britain.

The Kishorn yard has been building concrete production platforms since early on in the oil boom, and it's been a success, unlike other yards which opened only to close down. It is dwarfed by the hunched shoulder of Sgurr a' Chaorachain, the Peak of the Little Berries. Just to the left, the road snakes over the famous pass to Applecross, known as the Pass of the Cows, with gradients of one in four. Masochistic cyclists love it.

Motorists in Scotland have some fairly nerve-wracking hazards to negotiate, as these signs indicate . . .

If you were a motorist negotiating the single-track roads of the west coast in the old days, this was always a welcome sight – petrol pumps were few and far between. Today there is little need to worry. The roads have been widened, the petrol stations proliferate. But there is still something very reassuring about this lady in Kintail and her old-fashioned hand-operated pump. Only the price seems to have changed.

Dawn on Loch Carron, looking towards Loch Kishorn from the little village of Plockton, with its palm trees and bright colours. Plockton was one of the few happy things to emerge from the Clearances. It was laid out by Sir Hugh Innes to accommodate some of the victims. Today it is a tourist trap in summer, with a lively local regatta and even a nearby airstrip. In winter, however, too many of the houses are empty and dark.

Eilean Donan is the most photographed castle in Scotland, which may be why Douglas Corrance has allowed his shutter to stay open only long enough to catch its outline in the fading light. But everything about the Castle is spectacular: its position at the confluence of three lochs, Duich, Long and Alsh; its violent and romantic history as a Mackenzie seat; and its superb dimensions. Now massively restored, it looks today much as it must have done in medieval times when it was virtually unassailable.

The daunting aspect of the Cuillin Hills can be seen in this picture, taken from the east and the crofting community of Torrin. The water is the sea loch, Loch Slapin. As the clouds roll in the hills can turn bleak and treacherous within minutes. And if one of Skye's sudden mists descend, there is real danger for the amateur climber, "None but those monstrous creatures of God know how to join so much beauty with so much horror," wrote the poet Thomas Gray.

This is the northern end of the Cuillin ridge, with its highest peak on the left, Sgurr nan Gillean, 3,167 feet, the Peak of the Young Men. To the right is the sinisterly named Basteir group. The name is said to mean "executioner", but it is still a magnet to mountaineers, for whom the black gabbro rock is a delight to climb.

The Cuillin Hills, Skye, seen from the north. "I do not remember to have gone ten paces without an exclamation that there was no restraining," wrote Gray in 1765 after a Highland trip. "There are certain scenes that would awe an atheist into belief." One of these would certainly be the Cuillins, whose magic lies in their constantly changing shade, shape and colour in the Highland light.

On the beach outside Elgol primary school on Skye, the children grapple with a traditional skill – playing the chanter, the necessary first stage to the bagpipes. It would be a fairly safe bet to say these youngsters are Mackinnons. Of the thirteen pupils at Elgol school in 1982, no fewer than twelve were Mackinnons.

In these days when gathering in the hay is a routine business of stacking cuboid shapes on to a trailer, the ancient art of hay-making is a dying skill. Here, on Skye, it still thrives, however, although it is back-breaking work, and not always carried out under those brilliant blue skies.

From the Glenfinnan monument, looking southwest over Loch Shiel, its glassy surface a perfect reflection of the darkly tinged clouds above. Perfect – and yet the image on the water is not of quite the same quality. "Like – but oh how different!" as Wordsworth said of his mountain echo.

The statue of a kilted Highlander on top of the Glenfinnan monument at the head of Loch Shiel, where Charles Edward Stuart raised the (distinctly reluctant) clans on 19 August 1745. Cameron of Lochiel tried to persuade the Prince to call off the enterprise – without success. "Be the issue what it will," said the Prince, "I am determined to display my standard and take the field with such as may join it. Lochiel . . . may stay at home and learn his Prince's fate from the newspapers." Lochiel did no such thing. "I'll share the fate of my Prince," he said, "And so shall every man over whom nature or fortune hath given me any power."

The white sands of Morar, Inverness-shire. There is only one good reason why this is not, cannot be, and never will become the tropical paradise it poses as. That reason is the dark and lowering sky which is about to open and send the carefree couple skeetering back for shelter. But for this, the beach would be as crowded as Waikiki, and the Highlands would be ruined.

Conversation piece on the harbour at Mallaig, once the biggest herring fishing port in Europe, accounting for one third of all herring landed in Britain, with a fleet of up to a hundred boats. Mallaig rose to the occasion, building all the facilities necessary to exploit the trade, but overfishing and a lack of proper regulation led to a temporary ban, and Mallaig, like other ports, has had to switch to other fish, including mackerel and scampi. Unlike Ullapool, however, the "Klondikers", or big foreign boats coming in to trade, have not been a notable feature in Mallaig where tourism, deep-sea fishing and trips to the islands are a mainstay in the summer.

There are, of course, still good boats in Mallaig harbour. The one below is named after the Five Sisters of Kintail, the range of hills that dominates Loch Duich and Glenshiel to the north.

These fishing boats are at Tarbert, Loch Fyne, where they have been photographed (at no small risk) from atop a neighbouring boat. The bright colours and gleaming paint are typical of a place which is now more of a resort than a fishing village, within easy weekend reach of Glasgow. The creels on the decks suggest lobster and crab.

Ignoring the demands of geography, and in order to obtain a suitably aesthetic counterpoint to the shot on the left, the photographer has sprung deftly across to the east coast to capture fishing nets drying at Buckie on the Banffshire coast. Buckie is still a thriving fishing port with its own fleet which has adapted to the hazards of the modern fishing industry.

The stationmaster at Glenfinnan on the West Highland line, the most romantic stretch of railway in the world, summed up by the names of its stations – Locheilside, Glenfinnan, Lochailort, Beasdale, Arisaig, Morar, Mallaig. . . .

Note the machine on which the stationmaster is resting his arm.

This is where the "tablet" is inserted – a small disc carried from station to station by the engine driver, in a pouch attached to a large metal loop (there are two leaning against the wall behind the machine). The tablet is collected by the stationmaster, who thrusts his arm through the loop as the engine

pulls into the station, exchanging it simultaneously with another one. He retrieves the tablet, feeds it into the machine, and thus releases the signal at the next station. Until this is done, the train cannot proceed. Collisions on such single-track lines are thus avoided.

The great hump that is Ben Nevis,
Britain's highest mountain
(4,406 feet) although by no means
as spectacular as, say, Torridon.
There are easy ways up Ben Nevis
and there are hard ways, and true
mountaineers prefer the latter. It is
a sport that held few attractions for
Captain Burt on his travels in the
Highlands in 1730, and he did not
even like the scenery: "... the whole
of a dismal gloomy brown, drawing
upon a dirty purple; and most of all
disagreeable when the Heath is in
bloom ..." He described a group of
English officers setting out to climb
Ben Nevis, spending the entire day
from five in the morning to sunset
trying to do it, then failing "for bogs
and perpendicular rocks". When
they had got as high as they could,
they saw "nothing but the tops of
other mountains", which shows
that the sport has not changed in
essence in the last two hundred and
fifty years.

Loch Linnhe. An evening shot, with hay-rake. A scene worthy of Turner who was entranced by the peculiar and infinitely varying light of the northwestern Highlands. A more recent painter, the American artist Jon Schueler, wrote of it: "When I speak of nature I'm speaking of the sky, because in many ways the sky became nature to me. And when I think of the sky, I think of the Scottish sky . . . I found its convulsive movement and change and drama such a concentration of activity that it became all skies and even all nature to me."

A cast-iron milestone on the island of Mull.

Mull has two splendid castles which could hardly be more different. This is an autumn view from inside one of them – Torosay Castle, about a mile and a half south of Craignure. It is 19th century, although its terraced grounds, perhaps its best feature, were laid out by the great 20th-century architect, Sir Robert Lorimer, who believed in the perfect synthesis of a building with its surroundings. The other castle, Duart, is rather older – 600 years older in fact. It has been a Maclean stronghold virtually all that time.

Iona is just as hard to reach now as it was in St Columba's day, which may have been the reason it was chosen as a religious settlement. Its rocky outcrops, seen from the cockpit of the photographer's plane, show how difficult it must have been to land.

The little post office on Iona serves in winter an island community of around a hundred souls, but many hundreds more in summer, who come to stay at the monastery, or the retreat-house or simply to explore an island where forty-eight Scottish kings, including Duncan and Macbeth, are said to be buried. "That man is little to be envied whose patriotism would not gain force upon the plain of Marathon, or whose piety would not grow stronger amid the ruins of Iona," wrote Dr Johnson in 1773, although he noted then that the inhabitants were "remarkably gross and remarkably neglected", and that they had "no school for education nor temple for worship". Today, with the Iona Community thriving, thanks to Dr George (later Lord) MacLeod who founded it in 1938, the island is very much alive.

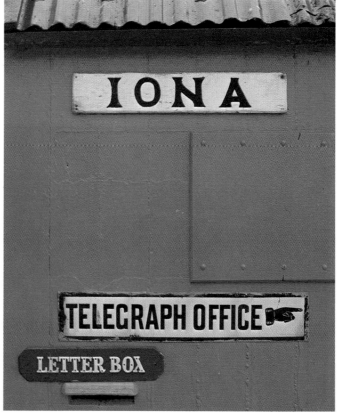

The colours of these sea-front houses in Tobermory, the main town of the island of Mull, are more Scandinavian than those of the East Neuk of Fife on the other side of Scotland, and there has been a little cheating – they were specially brightened up to appear in a film being shot there. The houses too are more imposing (I particularly like the Mishnish Hotel). Founded as a fishing port in the late 18th century, Tobermory's harbour is more widely used by yachtsmen or by treasure hunters who still believe that untold riches lie in the bay, where a Spanish galleon fleeing after the Armada was blown up in 1588 by a Mull man – one Donald Maclean. Not, it must be said, through any desire to help the English Queen, but because the Spanish sailors had failed to pay for the supplies they had taken on board.

On Islay the Bank of Scotland calls itself *Banca Na H-Alba*, though I note no attempt to render similarly "Eurocheque" or "Visa Card" – perhaps the concept of plastic money is alien to the Gaelic language. Islay had an important role in the development of Gaelic, for it was here that John Francis Campbell collected his *Popular Tales of the West Highlands*, whose publication in 1860 was largely responsible for the revival of interest in the language.

Port Ellen was laid out in the early 19th century by one of Islay's indigenous lairds, W. F. Campbell, also a noted Gaelic scholar. The steep street sloping down to the sea, with its huddled houses which look as if they might topple over one another into the water if given a shove, is in fact part of a sturdy and attractively designed little town.

Islay is famous for other things of course, notably its whisky; but for this girl taking her pony across the shallow waters off its coast, its main blessing is peace, space, and emptiness.

Islay's whiskies are not only deservedly famous, they have names that run smoothly off the tongue: Laphroaig, Lagavulin, Ardbeg, Coal Isla. . . . The picture shows a cooper tending some of the thousands of sherry casks where the whisky is put to mature and acquire its distinctive colour. I like the late Neil Gunn's picture of the wan poet Keats contemplating a whisky cask silently, until the friendly cask is driven to say: "Tak' a wee drop, laddie. God kens ye need it."

In the graveyard at Kilmartin, north of Lochgilphead, in Argyll, sits a man who, but for a kindly slant to the mouth, might be the grim reaper himself, sharpening his scythe in readiness for the next mortal soul on his endless list. In fact, it was the local grave-tender merely tidying up the graves, which include some Celtic slabs almost as old as Father Time himself.

Glencoe has many faces, but
Douglas Corrance has captured a
hitherto unsuspected Japanese
flavour in this calm, reflective view
of the Pap of Glencoe, taken from
the north side of Loch Leven. In the
centre of the loch is the island of
Eilean Munde, where generations of
Glencoe MacDonalds are buried.

Another stunning sunset, this time out over the island of Kerrera to Mull, with the town of Oban nestling beneath us. The straight V of the boat's wake on the bay reminds one of another quality of a Highland evening – the noise, or rather lack of it. Here, one can guess, there was only the putt-putt of the boat's engine to break the silence.

Sunset on a grey chilly evening on Campbeltown Loch, as a small yacht sets out to sea. It has left in its wake Davaar Island, where there is a deep cave with a painted crucifixion on the wall. It was executed in 1887 by a local man, Archibald Mackinnon, who said he had been told to do it in a dream.

Castle Stalker, a superb 15th-century tower house, recently restored, is set on an offshore rock at the mouth of Loch Laich. It was a Stewart stronghold, disputed for years and finally won by Campbells. It was nearly lost earlier on, when a Stewart of Appin, known as *Boathaire*, the "muddle-headed", swapped it for an eight-oared boat in the course of a drunken evening spent with a Campbell of Aird. The Stewarts never really accepted this; Castle Stalker was surrendered to the Earl of Argyll only in 1691 when it was used as a garrison to cut off the fleeing MacDonalds after the massacre of Glencoe.

A gothic shot of distinctly threatening Highland cattle with an unearthly sunset illuminating Glencoe behind them. We are in an area where the most famous of the Gaelic poets, Duncan Ban Macintyre, wrote many of his songs. '''S aobhach a'greigh uallach, 'N uair ghluaiseadh iad gu faramach'' run two of his lines: ''The gallant herd is joyous, as they move off with noisy stir''. Macintyre was a romantic poet, and only in the original can one capture the beauty of his lines. Rendered into English they tend to sound wooden or insipid.

The Three Sisters of Glencoe: Beinn Fhada, Gearr Aonach and Aonach Dubh, topped with snow. We are looking west up Glencoe towards the area where most of the notorious massacre took place on the night of 13 February 1692. Those MacDonalds who escaped (and most did) may well have come pouring down here to where three rivers meet.

We are in Campbell country. Inveraray Castle, glimpsed through stone balustrades, is the seat of the 12th Duke of Argyll, Chief of Clan Campbell. From this place, over some six hundred years of Scottish history, earls and dukes of Argyll have wielded what was, at times, great power. These days the power has gone, but for the thousands of tourists who visit the Castle, and in particular those bearing the name of Campbell, expectations remain high: they expect the Castle to look like a ducal seat; they expect the Duke to live in a manner in which they suppose dukes live; and they expect his castle still to look like the great stronghold of a great clan chief – which it does.

And the Duke himself, seated here at the head of the table. As Marquess of Lorne and Kintyre, Earl of Campbell and Cowal, Viscount Lochow and Glenyla, Baron Inverary, Mull, Morven and Tiry, Baron Campbell, Earl Argyll, Baron Lorne, Baron Kintyre, Baron Sunridge, Baron Hamilton of Hameldon, 36th Baron and 46th Knight of Lochow, Mac Cailein Mor, Chief of Clan Campbell, Hereditary Master of the Royal Household, Scotland, Hereditary High Sheriff of the County of Argyll, Admiral of the Western Coast and Isles, Keeper of the Great Seals of Scotland and of the Castles of Dunstaffnage, Dunoon, and Carrick and Tarbert, the 12th Duke has many roles to play. He appears to fill them admirably.

And those who come to see the show like to record what they see. This well-equipped visitor, with his Japanese cine camera and his otter-head sporran, is one of about 80,000 visitors who come to the Castle every year. There is a certain relentlessness about this man. He knows what he is after, and he is going to complain if he does not get it.

Beneath the Campbell tartan tablecloth and the Campbell tartan skirts, this Cairn terrier has spotted something she doesn't like the look of. Could it be a MacDonald?

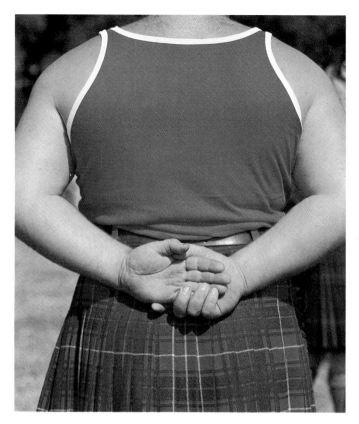

As children we missed much of the ritual of the annual Highland Games. We were too busy at the fairground outside the ring, spending sixpences furiously at the shooting gallery or getting sick on toffee apples. The "heavy" events were usually fairly late on, however, so we managed to catch them. The competitor above is at the Aboyne Games in Aberdeenshire. He will be preparing to toss the caber, throw the 56-pound weight over the bar, throw the hammer, or "putt" the shot. Often one man, a tower of strength, wins all these events to become the superhero of the day.

It's not only the competitors who dress up. These boys at Newtonmore on Speyside have been lovingly prepared for the Games, though they are only part of the audience. There is a slight disparity in the Highland dress. The standard rule is that the kilt should hang to about halfway down the kneecap, but judging from the chap in the middle, hemlines are going up at Newtonmore this season.

Judging a piping competition is an art in itself. It requires total concentration, an acute ear, and an intimate knowledge of that most arcane music form, pibroch. The judges take their work seriously. At a nationwide competition recently, where the best pipers in the country were participating, the first prize was simply not given because the judges decided that no one had come up to the standard that Scottish piping demands. Here, at the Islay Games, the judge may be a bit more lenient, but the attention given to this young competitor is every bit as great.

Four stewards studying the fine print at the Aboyne Games. Seasoned as they clearly are, there is an obvious error to be spotted amongst them: one golden rule is of paramount importance for the kilt-wearer – to adopt a delicate sitting position. The gentleman on the right has broken this rule . . . to an almost embarrassing extent.

These little girls at the Glenfinnan Games in Inverness-shire are preparing to compete in a sword dance, a Highland fling, or perhaps even a sailor's hornpipe. They have probably been preparing for this moment all year, and they will be judged on an intricate series of rules relating to steps and pointed feet and perfectly held hands. It is an esoteric art, a parody, some would say, of Scottish dancing, but it's always one of the day's most popular events.

In the field events at Highland Games, more modern gear is beginning to challenge the supremacy of the tartan. This shot, at the Aboyne Games, shows a clear contrast in styles. The contestants are often "on tour", travelling from games to games during the summer season to compete for modest prizes.

Throwing the weight, again at Aboyne. Despite its potential inconvenience, the kilt is still more or less *de rigueur* at these events. What is worn under it is hardly a matter of speculation for anyone who takes more than a casual interest, as the picture clearly indicates.

The *Waverley* paddle steamer is the only ocean-going paddle steamer in the world, though these days it ventures little into the ocean. You are likely to find it in Ayr, from where it takes safe trips up and down the Clyde, belching great clouds of black smoke.

The Gourock ferry pulling into Dunoon, Argyll, probably Glasgow's favourite holiday resort. Like all pier resorts, Dunoon has seen better, more glamorous days, but it's still a tried and trusted favourite

Castle Campbell, or Castle Gloom as it is sometimes known, overlooks Dollar Glen with a superb view south to the Firth of Forth. It has a 14th-century square tower joined to a 16th-century wing, and was one of the many strongholds sacked by Montrose in his war of attrition against the government and Clan Campbell, a war in which Campbell territory was ravished and the clan came close to annihilation.

The Grand Match on the Lake of Menteith (the only *lake* in Scotland) is one of the great – and rare – sights of Scotland. It takes place only in the coldest of winters when the ice on the Lake has reached a sufficient depth to support the weight of more than a thousand players. When it has, the call goes out for curlers to compete in a "bonspiel", as the match is known in curling parlance, between Scotland North and Scotland South. It's happened two or three times in the last dozen years. This is what it looks like when it does. A stone has been "laid", and from now on its progress is up to the sweepers who, to the shouted command "Soop, soop!" will polish the ice furiously to melt the top micromillimetre and so speed the stone up – or they will stand back if it is going well. Out of sight are a few bottles of medicinal Scotch, an essential accompaniment to the game since it keeps out the cold. Especially helpful to kilt-wearers.

Stirling University was founded in 1967 – the first completely new one to be built in Scotland for almost 400 years. James VI promised Stirling he would give the town a "free college", but did nothing about it. The 20th-century version is set in 300 acres of landscaped parkland, including this 23-acre loch where the students can sail right in the middle of the campus. Stirling had a reputation for radicalism, not to say dissidence, amongst its students in the early seventies, but it has built a solid reputation, particularly in the sciences, and carries out important research work in electronic and ecological studies.

Before the supremacy of Edinburgh, Stirling was virtually the capital of Scotland, and the Castle, seen here behind some truculent Blue-Grey stirks (or bullocks), was the royal residence. It is every bit as impressive in situation as Edinburgh, commanding breathtaking views over Lowlands and Highlands, while the River Forth coils east and west over flat meadows beneath. What are now the barracks were James III's Parliament Hall, and beside it James V built a palace in Renaissance style. There is a sally-port through which James V used to venture in disguise to talk to the townspeople; and a peephole through which Mary Queen of Scots looked out over the town before her departure to France.

Very much a 19th-century example of a Scottish hero: the explorer David Livingstone, whose memorial stands in his home town of Blantyre, Lanarkshire. His explorations aroused enormous enthusiasm in his native land, and he was feted each time he returned, but he himself was a tortured man who felt that he never received the backing he deserved from the British government. In the end, his setbacks and his illnesses in Africa make any account of his life painful reading.

Robert the Bruce's great achievement was not only to unite Scotland, but to renew a sense of nationhood. This statue, erected in 1964, stands in Stirlingshire on the site of Bannockburn, a brilliantly executed battle. But it is arguable that Bruce's later success owed as much to the weakness of Edward II of England as to any special ability to hold Scotland together. It was very soon after his death that the country was once more plunged into civil strife, with the succession as uncertain as ever.

Showing a fine sense of priorities, the former owner of this house near Inverness has set two figures into his wall. The one on the left is William Wallace, on the right Admiral Nelson. Nelson is hardly a Scottish hero, but he shared some of the fighting qualities of William Wallace, whom Lewis Grassic

Gibbon hailed as "one of the few authentic national heroes; authentic in the sense that he apprehended and moulded the historic forces of his time in a fashion denied to all but a few of the world's great political leaders – Cromwell, Lincoln, Lenin."

A perfectly symmetrical series of ploughed furrows. The isolated farmhouse and the flatness of the landscape suggest Holland rather than central Scotland, but beyond it the cliffs drop in a way that cliffs never do on the Zuider Zee. Note the straw, baled in the modern fashion by binding into huge Swiss rolls, ready to be lifted bodily by fork lift and driven away.

The Pineapple at Dunmore, Stirlingshire, is an 18th-century folly, but a functional one: here pineapples were actually grown. The main structure is 45 feet high and was originally a garden retreat. Restored by the Landmark Trust, it is available for holidays in decidedly unusual surroundings.

Grangemouth is Scotland's biggest, indeed only, oil refinery, handling petrochemicals for BP and ICI and on the point of accepting butane and propane gas by pipeline from Mosmorran on the Forth. Industrially it is in good shape. Environmentally it is causing growing concern. Not only is the nearby River Carron badly polluted, but the sheer accumulation of noxious and explosive substances in one place is a risky proposition.

This picture of Loch Lomond, with cattle and children, is in the nature of a send-up of all those chocolate-box picture postcards of the Highlands, which are nothing like the real thing but are still the ones everyone wants to buy. Doubtless this one would sell like hot cakes . . .

These tall houses in the cotton-milling village of New Lanark were part of a chapter in social history that went far beyond the confines of southern Scotland. They were model houses, managed by the great Welsh social reformer Robert Owen as part of his successful drive to improve labour conditions in the cotton industry. Today they are being restored again by a more middle-class type of resident (I doubt if Owen's millworkers could have run to the flashy car in the foreground).

"And through my heart, as through
a dream,
Flows on that black disdainful
stream . . .
Alexander Smith's epic poem about
Victorian Glasgow evoked a sinister
picture of the Clyde – the "long dark
river of the dead". But although the
Clyde can be as gloomy as any other
river at night, it is never less than
majestic. The great shipbuilding
days are over, and other heavy
industries have declined, but it is
still Glasgow's lifeblood. As the old
saying goes, "Glasgow made the
Clyde, and the Clyde made
Glasgow".

The University of Glasgow and
Kelvingrove Park seen beneath a
delicate blanketing of snow.
Scotland's second oldest
university, founded in 1451, has
always been a "civic" college – one
that draws its students from the
area – and its strength since the
19th century has lain in its
engineering faculties as well as in
law and medicine. It houses the
Hunterian Museum which for a
while had a windfall on its hands –
the copyright in all the furniture
designs of Charles Rennie
Mackintosh, whose work is
enormously popular.

I do not know why there should be four bobbies waiting at the other end of "the Suspension Bridge", as it is known. The whole point about Glasgow these days is that it is supposed to be very far from the crime-ridden, gang-ruled place we've all been brought up to believe is the real thing. You can even walk through the Gorbals, they say, without noticing you're there. But I dare say they still need a few policemen, just in case. . . .

Glasgow Cathedral is the only large Scottish church, apart from St Magnus Cathedral in Kirkwall, to have survived the Reformation virtually intact. The craftsmen of Glasgow are said to have banded together to prevent its destruction. The founding of the Cathedral, and the consecration of Glasgow's first bishop – John Achaius – in 1114, are two of the earliest recorded facts about the city.

Jewish ex-servicemen gather for Remembrance Day. Glasgow's Jewish population was never large – it did not compare to the number of Irish – but it made an important contribution to the city by providing the services which sustained its progress. Unlike so many European countries, Scotland seems not to have been tainted by anti-semitism. Amongst Glasgow's more celebrated Jewish sons: Sir Isaac Wolfson, Sir Monty Finnieston, Chaim Berant, Jeremy Isaacs, Benno Schotz.

Glasgow Museum and Art Gallery at Kelvingrove has what is possibly the best municipal collection of pictures in Britain. It also has superb displays of sculpture, jewellery, silver and ceramics. It cannot do much, however, to prevent young children from wandering around in electric-blue anoraks which clash horribly with the fine paintings of Signor Bellini and pupils.

They say you can tell if a Glasgow family is on the way up if (a) they live in a tenement faced in red sandstone; (b) a tenement with a tiled close; (c) a tenement with a tiled close and doors. Judging by this one off Byres Road in the city's west end, the families here have a wee bit to go yet.

West passes East in a Glasgow street. There is a sizeable Indian and Pakistani population in the city, partly, it is said, because in the fifties and sixties, job scouts for Glasgow transport went east looking for potential employees as drivers and conductors on the buses, while those from London went west.

Sir William Burrell gave his astonishing art collection to the City of Glasgow in 1944. It has taken 39 years to find and open a home for it, but now the Burrell Collection can finally be seen in this new and remarkable gallery in Pollok Park. In his lifetime Burrell surrounded himself with art and artefacts from all over the world and from every period. By the time of his death in 1958, he had bequeathed some 8,000 items to Glasgow, but because of his stringent conditions about where they should be housed, no suitable place had been found by the time he died. Now it has, and the result is an impressive tribute to one of the greatest cultural benefactors Scotland has ever had.

Shipbuilding in Glasgow has become a victim of the biggest world slump in the industry since the 1930s. It has meant massive redundancies, the closing of yards, and cutthroat competition. The faces of these three workers at a Govan yard reflect perhaps the uncertainty of their profession.

"The majority of Glasgow pubs are for connoisseurs of the morose..." said Hugh McDiarmid sourly, "We have no damned fellow-feeling at all." The two gentlemen sharing a pint in the Toll Bar presumably disagree. They seem to be keeping their moroseness well under control – at least for the time being.

The *Glasgow Herald* calls itself "Scotland's Newspaper", but it is very much a product of the Strathclyde area, catering for the Glasgow businessman – a solid paper. It is also the oldest newspaper in Britain and has just celebrated its two hundredth anniversary.

The steel tracery of two giant cranes at Port Glasgow is elegantly parodied by the wrought iron of Victorian streetlamps. There were four separate ports serving the city – Glasgow itself, Port Dundas at the Glasgow end of the Forth and Clyde canal, and Greenock and Port Glasgow on the Firth of Clyde. Port Glasgow has been outgrown by Greenock but is still important as a shipbuilding town.

ENQUIRIES

The genius of Charles Rennie Mackintosh: the restored dining room from Mackintosh's home, now part of the Hunterian Museum which belongs to the University of Glasgow; the exterior of The Hill House, Helensburgh, which Mackintosh designed in its entirety and which now belongs to the National Trust for Scotland; a detail of window catches at The Hill House; curtains and a table at The Hill House; and the hallway of Glasgow School of Art, a Mackintosh design.

Charles Rennie Mackintosh died in poverty in 1928, bitter about his lack of recognition. Since then his reputation as an original architect and designer has grown steadily, until today his pieces command respectful space in any anthology and record prices whenever they turn up in the salerooms. A desk designed by him for his own use recently fetched £80,000, a world record for a piece of 20th-century furniture. His themes are crispness, elegance, strong contrasts in colour, lightness and simplicity. He was recognized and hailed abroad – particularly in Vienna – but only now has Glasgow fully come to terms with the fact that it had a genius on its hands.

Rothesay on the island of Bute, wearing a tropical look and resembling not a bit the seaside resort made famous by Willie Miller's old folksong, which begins:
"One Hogmanay at Glesca Fair,
There was me mysel' and several mair,
And we a' went off tae ha'e a tear,
And spend the nicht in Rothesay-O"
And has somewhere in it:
"We a' lay doon to tak our case,
When somebody happened for to sneeze,
And he wakened half a million fleas
In a lodging hoose in Rothesay-O."
But I dare say things have changed since then.

The railway station at Wemyss Bay, embarkation point for Arran, Bute, and, of course, Rothesay-O. It is a marvellous example of railway architecture, its Edwardian elegance a reminder of more confident days. But they still take a pride in its appearance, as the banked potted plants show.

144

Sunset at Largs on the Ayrshire coast, today a holiday resort but still remembered every year for the great Battle of Largs in 1263, which threw off the Viking yoke and won for Scotland control of the Hebrides and the Isle of Man. There is a nine-day festival every September to commemorate the battle which actually took place in October, Alexander III having deliberately delayed the engagement to take advantage of the autumn gales.

Lochranza Castle on the island of Arran in the Forth of Clyde is a splendid ruin dating from the 16th or 17th century, but there was an earlier building here in the 12th century. It is one of the many castles where Robert the Bruce is said to have stayed after hiding out as an outlaw on Arran and on Rathlin Island, where, of course, he watched the spider spin its web and persuade him that it might after all be worth returning to the mainland to try once again to roll back the English might.

The steep hills of Arran, viewed
from Bute over the heads of a
baleful-looking heifer and her calf.
Arran is a good place for stiff
walking or hill climbing, though you
can cross it perfectly easily by
means of a road called the String.

Ailsa Craig, off the Ayrshire coast, is an uncompromising sort of rock, solid, volcanic, around 1,000 feet high, peopled by sea birds. There is a nice west coast legend about the rock, involving a rather stupid water spirit who lived on Arran, where she herded cattle. The people of Arran wanted to give her a suit of clothes, which offended her so much she decided to leave. She stepped onto Ailsa Craig, but as she waited, one foot still on Arran, a three-masted ship passing by knocked her into the sea, and she drowned. There is a Gaelic saying about such women: "She was out on the knoll when wisdom was distributed. . . ."

A misty view of Ayr with the neo-classical Town Hall spire and the New Bridge merging into the River Ayr. Burns wrote a dialogue for the New Bridge and the Auld Brig, just upriver, which reminds one of the rivalry between the rivers Don and Dee: the New Brig calls the Auld a "poor narrow foot-path of a street Where twa wheel-barrows tremble when they meet". The Auld Brig ripostes, ". . . tho' wi' crazy eild [old age] I'm sair forfairn, I'll be a brig when ye're a shapeless cairn!" The Auld Brig was right: the New Bridge is the third on its site. But the Auld Brig too has suffered with age: it can carry pedestrians only.

The bust of James Boswell in the former chapel at Auchinleck, the Boswell family home. Boswell's uncertain reputation as a literary figure in his own right, rather than just as Dr Johnson's biographer, is the fault of the historian Thomas Macauley who called him a "bigot and a sot". That view has been substantially revised, but Boswell did write of himself:
"So not a bent sixpence cares he Whether *with* him or *at* him you laugh"

Every year the tourists pour into the cottage in Alloway, Ayrshire, where Robert Burns was born . . .

. . . and down the road, in a souvenir shop in Alloway, postcards and models of Tam O'Shanter and Soutar Johnnie help to keep the Burns industry going.

And in the churchyard at Kirkoswald, the gravestones of "Tam O'Shanter" and Burns's schoolmaster are carefully labelled. But the Burns industry depends on a myth that bears very little relation to reality. Burns is presented as a bawdy, hard-drinking common man, no better nor worse than you

or me, but a fellow who could string together a few rollicking lines, or maybe bring a tear to the eye when the occasion demands.

As Edwin Muir, a fellow-poet, pointed out some fifty years ago, there is in the myth "no fundamental resemblance to Burns himself. Burns was not, for the age

he lived in, an immoderate drinker; nor was he a careless lover, and he perpetually cursed the weakness in himself which his admirers glorify. He had, like all poets of equal greatness, a keen and sure moral sense fed by a universal human sympathy such as no other Scotsman has possessed. His life

was not a happy one, but filled with misery and disappointment, which he bore bravely . . ."

Ah, but would the tourists go for it?

"Take the stomach of a sheep and wash it well. Leave it to soak for several hours in cold, salt water. Then turn out and pour scalding water on it and scrape with a knife. Now clean a sheep's pluck well. Pierce the heart and liver in several places, then boil the liver and lights for an hour and a half. When these have been boiled for 15 minutes change the water, and during the last half-hour let the pluck be boiled with them. Trim away the skins and discard any discoloured parts. Grate half the liver and mince all the rest finely. Add a pound of finely shredded meat, two chopped onions, half a nutmeg, grated, and a pinch of cayenne pepper. Moisten with half a pint of good gravy and juice of small lemon. Put the mixture into the bag prepared for it. Allow for swelling in cooking. Sew up securely and plunge into boiling water. Boil gently for three hours. Prick at times with a needle to let air out. Serve hot at once."

Traditional Scotch recipe

The kipper is as treasured a Scottish delicacy as the haggis and, dare I say it, a great deal more enjoyable. Bought lightly salted and properly smoked over oak chips, the flesh firm and plump and easing gently off the backbone, there is nothing to beat it. Except, perhaps, one of those excellent fish cakes.

Culzean Castle in Ayrshire, viewed from below the cliffs which give it one of the most striking prospects of any Scottish castle. Add to that the mastery of Robert Adam who virtually rebuilt it in the 1780s, and the result is a remarkable building.

Robert Adam's most imaginative addition was this great oval staircase, which he built onto the well of the Castle and between two ends of it. He supervised all the details, including the colour for the decor.

A good Wigtownshire face – on the harbour at Whithorn.

Still life with policeman's hat, viewed through a window in Port Logan, Wigtownshire. If there is a certain severity in the design, then that is entirely appropriate to this part of Scotland with its stern Presbyterian traditions.

A rudimentary milestone in Wigtownshire.

Set in the middle of the Glenkiln estate in Galloway, Henry Moore's King and Queen command the rolling landscape at their feet. They seem more at home here than in the confines of a gallery, as do others by Rodin, Epstein and Renoir, which stand nearby.

The Isle of Whithorn near the southernmost tip of Wigtownshire, in that area known as the Machars, is the place where, 397 years after the birth of Christ, St Ninian brought Christianity for the first time to Scotland. Ninian was a local man who went to Rome on a pilgrimage and returned here to build a little church of white plaster. The Venerable Bede called it "Candida Casa", hence "huit aern", hence Whithorn.

Three doves, in perfect formation, pose on a "doocot", or dovecote, at Ardwell on the Mull of Galloway. There are elaborate and fanciful doocots all over Scotland, and their purpose was not entirely decorative. Pigeons provided food in winter, dung as fertilizer or to make gunpowder, and there was an ancient belief that you would never die as long as pigeon feathers were used in your pillow.

Nearby, just north of Port Logan, are Logan Gardens – a tropical garden with rare shrubs, tree-ferns and the Brazilian *Gunnera Manicata*, the largest-leafed outdoor plant to grow in Britain – all benefitting from the mild Gulf Stream climate which plants enjoy, but which humans still find perishing cold.

If there is a touch of art nouveau about this door in Kirkcudbright, the old capital of that area known as the Stewartry, then that may be a reflection of Kirkcudbright's former reputation as an art colony. It is still a place where antique and craft shops jostle each other in the distinctive L-shaped High Street.

Not so far away, in the villages of Moniaive and Penpont in Dumfriesshire, artistic self-expression has found an outlet in these two houses. There might be a few raised eyebrows over the violently clashing green fence and railings, but there can be no question about the loving care devoted to the sweet peas.

Cattle prices have not always been to the liking of farmers in recent years, and this could account for the distinct air of despondency in the faces of these three locals at an auction in Newton Stewart in Wigtownshire.

Taking the plunge: down below is Portpatrick, the main holiday resort on the Rhinns of Galloway, the double peninsula that forms the far southwest corner of Scotland. You can almost throw a stone from here to Northern Ireland, although the main port across the channel is nowadays at Stranraer.

The old Ruthwell Parish Bank whose strongbox (with the emphasis on "strong" – note the padlocks) goes back to the days of Dr Henry Duncan, minister at Ruthwell (pronounced "Rivvel"), who founded the Savings Bank movement. There is a cottage in this Dumfriesshire village which became, in 1810, the first bank of this kind.

The Midsteeple of Dumfries with its offices, courthouse and prison. There is a decidedly un-Scottish look about all this – perhaps it is the cherub about to dispose of the crocodile – reminding one of a Flemish marketplace. We are not out of Burns country yet, for here he died. The citizens of Dumfries were proud of him and lined the streets for his funeral. "Who dae ye think'll be oor poet noo?" said one old man. Yet when a meeting was held to discuss a monument to the immortal memory, three people turned up, and it took thirty years to raise the £3,000 required. Most of the money came from England.

"Still were the fowlis flees in the air,
All stock and cattle seysit in their
   lair,
And everything, whareso them likis
   best
Bownis to tak the halesome nichtis
   rest
After the dayis labour and the heat"

The prologue to Bishop Gavin
Douglas of Dunkeld's 16th-century
translation of *The Aeneid*, from which
this passage is taken, provides a
finishing touch to the dying
moments of a summer's evening on
Skye.